The Academypreneur's Playbook: Turn Knowledge into a Revenue-Generating School

Your Step-by-Step Guide to Building a Profitable Private Training School

Dr. Constance Santego

Maximillian Enterprises
Kelowna, BC

The Academypreneur's Playbook: Turn Knowledge into a Revenue-Generating School

Copyright © 2025 by Constance Santego.

Copy Editor & Interior Design: Constance Santego
Book Layout: ©2017 BookDesignTemplates.com

Ordering Information:
Quantity sales. Special discounts are available on quantity purchases by corporations, associations, and others. Contact the "Special Sales Department" at the address below for details.

Trade Paperback ISBN: 978-1-990062-75-9
eBook ISBN: 978-1-990062-76-6
Created and published In Canada. Printed and bound in the United States of America

First Edition
Published by Maximillian Enterprises
Kelowna, BC
Canada
www.constancesantego.ca

ALSO BY DR. CONSTANCE SANTEGO

NOVELS

Illegitimate Grace

Okanagan Trilogy:
Beneath the Vineyards
Under the Okanagan Sun
Guardian of the Lake

The Nine Spiritual Gifts Series:
Journey of a Soul – (Vol 1 Michael)
Language of a Soul – (Vol 2 Gabriel)
Prophecy of a Soul – (Vol 3 Bath Kol)
Healing of a Soul – (Vol 4 Raphael)
Miracles of a Soul – (Vol 5 Hamied)
Knowledge of a Soul – (Vol 6 Raziel)
Wisdom of a Soul – (Vol 7 Uriel)
Faith of a Soul – (Vol 8 Pistis Sophia)

NONFICTION

The Intuitive Life, The Gift Of Prophecy, Third Edition
Fairy Tales, Dreams And Reality… Where Are You On Your Path? Second Edition
Your Persona… The Mask You Wear
Archangel Michael's Soul Retrieval Guide
Tesla And The Future Of Energy Medicine
Beyond Tesla: *Advancing The Science Of Energy Healing*
Tesla's Code: *Mastering Energy, Frequency, And Creative Power*
Beyond the Mind: *Harnessing the Power of Astral Projection for Creative Awakening*
Bend, Don't Break: *Finding Your Way Back to Abundance*
Ring Therapy: *A Guide to Healing and Balance*
Ring Therapy Pocket Guide
Floraopathy™: *The Art and Science of Vibrational Healing with Essential Oils*
Dear Older Me: *A Memoir… of Sorts*
It's Just Like Poker: *A Spiritual Guide to Playing the Cards Life Deals You*
Dear Older Me: A Memoir…*of Sorts*
AuricIons: *Unlocking Subconscious Healing Through Quantum Medicine*
More Than Bloodlines: *A Companion Book to AuricIons*

REIKI WISDOM, SERIES:

Angelic Lifestyle, a Vibrant Lifestyle
Angelic Lifestyle 42-Day Energy Cleanse
Reiki and the Power of The Joint Points: *Unlocking Energy Pathways for Healing* (Vol I)
Reiki and Karmic Healing: *Releasing Patterns From Past Lives* (Vol II)
Reiki and the Five Elements (Vol III)
Secrets of a Healer, Magic Of Reiki
The Reiki Master's Manual

SECRETS OF A HEALER, SERIES:
Magic Of Aromatherapy (Vol I)
Magic Of Reflexology (Vol II)
Magic Of The Gifts (Vol III)
Magic Of Muscle Testing (Vol IV)
Magic Of Iridology (Vol V)
Magic Of Massage (Vol VI)
Magic Of Hypnotherapy (Vol VII)
Magic Of Reiki (Vol VIII)
Magic Of Advanced Aromatherapy (Vol IX)
Magic Of Esthetics (Vol X)
The Reiki Master's Manual (Vol XI)

ADULT COLORING JOURNALS

SERIES-ZEN COLORING:
Quantum Energy and Mindful Living Journal (Vol 1)
Reiki Energy Journal (Vol 2)
Nine Spiritual Gifts Journal (Vol 3)
I Forgive Journal (Vol 4)

FOR CHILDREN
I am Big Tonight. I Don't Need the Light

COOKBOOK
My Favorite Recipes, with a Hint of Giggle

BUISNESS
Scaling Beyond 6 Figures: *Strategies For Health & Wellness Professionals*
How To Use ChatGPT For Authors: From Idea To Published Book

Dedication

To every dreamer who ever wondered,
"Could I really teach this?"—
Yes, you can.

To the students who taught me just as much as I ever taught
them,
and to the teachers who lit the way when I was finding my own
path—
this book is for you.

And to my family—who stood by me through every bold
decision, every detour, and every rebirth—
your belief carried me.

May this book spark the legacy you were born to leave.

"Education is not the filling of a pail, but the lighting of a fire."
— *William Butler Yeats*

Preface

I never set out to be a teacher—let alone the founder of an accredited college.

Back in 1999, I simply wanted to open a healing center. I envisioned a space where I could see clients, teach a few classes, and offer products that supported holistic wellness. But when I walked into City Hall to apply for a business license, everything changed.
They told me **no**.

I was stunned. I had already signed a lease. I had a vision. But it was the man behind the counter who changed my life with five words:
"Then you're a school, right?"

And just like that… I became one.

From that unexpected moment forward, I navigated the maze of turning knowledge into education, courses into programs, and students into practitioners. I built a school—one that would eventually be government-accredited, audited annually, and known for launching thousands of global graduates into successful holistic and esthetic careers.

But I also made mistakes—some big enough to cost me financially, emotionally, and legally.

This book isn't just a how-to manual. It's a real-world roadmap built on experience, both the inspiring wins and the humbling lessons. Whether you're a practitioner who wants to teach what you know, or a passionate educator trying to understand the rules and realities of launching your own school—this book is here to guide you.

If you've ever wondered:
"Can I really teach this?"
"Is it legal?"
"What makes something a *real* school?"
"Where do I even start?"

This book is for you.

Let's begin—together.

Dr. Constance Santego
Ph.D., Doctorate in Natural Medicine, College Founder, Bestselling Author

"The meaning of life is to find your gift. The purpose of life is to give it away."
— Pablo Picasso

Contents

Dedication viii

Preface x

Introduction 1

    Why You Can Start a School—Even Without a Degree
in Education 1

    The Truth: Anyone Can Teach… But Teaching Well—
And Legally—is a Different Matter 4

    What Does It Really Mean to Be a Teacher? 6

    What You'll Gain from This Book 10

Part 1: Your Knowledge Is Enough *(If You Structure It Right)*
.... 12

Chapter 1: From Passion to Program 13

    Who Can Teach Legally? (The Real Answer) 13

    The Misconception 14

    All About the Post-Secondary Teacher's Diploma 15

    Instructor Certification: Regulated vs. Unregulated
Courses 21

    To Register Your Course/Program or Not 28

    When Regulation Comes Into Play 30

    Owning Your Courses vs. Teaching Someone Else's 32

    Accreditation Rules on Curriculum Ownership 34

    Step-by-Step Guide: Teacher to School Founder 38

Chapter 2: Who Owns the School? 46

Understanding Ownership Models: Sole Proprietor, Partnership, or Corporation 46

Accreditation & Legal Responsibilities by Ownership Type 49

The Money: Who's Paying and For What? 50

Personal vs. Business Bank Accounts 54

Changing Structures (Sole Proprietor → Incorporated → Accredited) 56

Holding Tuition in Trust Until Earned 57

Contracts, Refund Rules & When Tuition Becomes the School's 60

How Time Affects Refunds in Regulated Programs 64

Refund Tied to "Time Allowed" to Complete, Not Actual Access 66

Intake Forms, Consent Forms & Communication 70

Chapter 3: Course Creation Basics 74

Turning Your Method Into Teachable Modules 74

The 3 Pillars of a Good Course: Learning Outcomes, Assessment, Structure 78

Hours-Based vs. Outcome-Based Learning 82

What Is Hours-Based Learning? 82

What Is Outcome-Based Learning? 83

Online Platform & EdTech Tools: Choosing the Right System for Your School 86

PDFs, Videos, Assignments – How Much Is Enough? 89

Certification vs. Education: What's the Difference—and Where Does Your Course Fit? 93

Chapter 4: Building Your Curriculum – Course by Course, Year by Year..97

Single Courses (Certificates) 97

Diploma Program Structure (Yearly Levels)................98

Courses Within Programs 99

Shared Core Courses Within Multi-Certificate Programs 101

Using Academic Titles: Bachelor's, Master's, Doctorate, and Ph.D.. 104

To Become a University 108

To Become a College.. 111

Are Unregistered "Colleges" Legal? 116

Course Credits for Associations: What You Need to Know... 119

Owning the Course vs. Teaching Another's.............. 121

Who Can Register Courses with Professional Associations?... 123

Chapter 5: Student Experience = Your Reputation 126

Student Expectations & Results: What Are They Really Getting? 126

Designing Transformation, Not Just Information...... 128

Why Good Teaching Changes Lives—Not Just Minds 129

Understanding Adult Learning Styles....................... 133

The Power of Feedback Loops 135

Motivation: Why Adults Actually Stick With It........ 136

Checklist for Enrolling International Students 137

Why Should They Choose *Your* School? Questionnaire
.... 140

Part 2: The Legal & Business Side of Starting a School....143

Chapter 6: Name Search.. 144

The Importance of Choosing the Right Name for Your
School or Program 144

Double-Check: Is Your Name or Acronym Already
Taken?.. 146

Common Terms for Educational Institutions............. 149

Registering Your School Name: Provincial/State vs.
National Considerations 155

Federal/National Name Registration........................ 156

Legal Name Registration vs Trademark: What's the
Difference?.. 157

Chapter 7: What Makes It a "School" Legally?.....................164

Do You Need a Physical Location? 164

City Business Licensing.. 168

Zoning and Inspections 173

When a "Workshop" Becomes a "School" 177

Chapter 8: Certificates, Diplomas & Accreditation 180

The Truth Behind Those Words................................ 180

Provincial/National Association Rules 183

What Are Associations and Why Do They Matter?... 183

When Do You Need a Teaching Credential?............. 187

Teacher Contracts & Intellectual Property Clauses:
Protecting Your School and Your Content 190

Is Government Accreditation Necessary?................. 194

Chapter 9: Insurance & Licensing for You and Your Students
....208

Insurance Requirements for Schools: Beyond Basic
Liability.. 208

What Your Students Need to Get Insurance and a
Business Licence.. 214

When Students *Cannot* Legally Get a Licence.......... 216

Working with Associations (or Creating Your Own
Standards) 219

Part 3: Running & Growing Your Private Training School
....226

Chapter 10: Setting Up the School Space............................227

Renting vs. Home-Based vs. Shared Space 227

Required Equipment and Legal Considerations 231

Disability & Accessibility Compliance: Creating
Inclusive Learning Spaces (Online and Off) 234

Long-Term Record Keeping: The 55-Year Requirement
.... 238

Homework, Written Exams & Hosting Practical
Sessions.. 244

Chapter 11: Enrollment, Marketing & Messaging.................248

Setting Fair Tuition... 248

Fair Tuition for International Students 251

International Student Tuition Policies in Canada 253

Clear Refund Policies And Contracts 256

Marketing Compliance & Ethical Advertising for
Private Training Schools... 259

Building Trust: Your Bio, Reviews & Testimonials . 262

Handling Complaints & Student Disputes: Protecting Your School with Transparency & Process 265

Chapter 12: Scaling, Auditing & Legacy 269

What It Takes to Get Audited or Accredited 269

Delivery Formats: Online, Hybrid, Hobby, ... 273

Registration vs. Accreditation 276

(Same Association, Different Levels) 276

When You're Exempt: Understanding "Recreational," "Hobby," or "Non-Vocational" Training 278

Are Core Courses Included in the 40-Hour / $4,000 PTIB Threshold? 281

Growing into a Multi-Instructor or Franchised Model 286

Licensing or Certifying Others to Teach Your Program 287

Franchising Your School Model 288

Selling or Licensing Your Course Materials 290

Exit Strategy for School Owners: Planning for What's Next 293

Reactivation or Dormancy Rules for Closed or Paused Schools 300

Chapter 13: How to Avoid Failure and Bankruptcy 304

Lessons Learned the Hard Way—So You Don't Have To 304

The Biggest Mistakes New School Owners Make 304

Cross-Provincial Compliance & Legal Risks 308

Moving or Sharing Student Files Without Permission Is Illegal 311

My Cautionary Tale: When Passion Meets Paperwork
.... 314

Final Thoughts: Your Legacy Begins Now 318

Appendix.. 322

Regulated Courses/Programs 322

Bibliography 376

About The Author 378

Message from the Author.. 380

"Legacy is not leaving something for people. It's leaving something in people."

— *Peter Strople*

The *Academypreneur's* Playbook: Turn Knowledge into a Revenue-Generating School

Introduction

Why You Can Start a School—Even Without a Degree in Education

I never set out to become a teacher—let alone the owner of an accredited college. Honestly, if you had told me that back in the late '90s, I would have laughed. Loudly.

But sometimes life doesn't ask for your permission. It just hands you a new path.

In 1999, I left my job and decided to follow my passion. I signed a lease on a starter space with promise space where I envisioned creating a healing center. My dream? A welcoming storefront with a small retail section, a private room to see clients, and a cozy space to hold meetings and classes. Simple. Honest. Heart-centered.

Then came my first reality check.

I walked into City Hall to get my business licence. The clerk looked at me, then at my application, and said, "No."

Just... no.

I stood there in shock. My mind raced—*What do you mean no? I already signed a one-year lease!* I must have looked completely stunned because a man from the office eventually walked over and asked what was going on. The clerk explained what I wanted to do.

He looked at her, then said something that changed the course of my entire life:

"She's a school."

With that, he walked away. The clerk began typing again as if this sudden plot twist made perfect sense.

I asked, "Wait—what does that mean?"

She replied, "As long as you are what you say you are, you're fine."

I blinked. "So… what do I do next?"

She said, "Pay for the business licence and make sure you're a school when the inspection happens."

I paid the fee, left the office, and drove straight to my mom's shop—conveniently located next to my new space. I walked in, looked at her, and said:

"I'm a school."

No plan. No curriculum. Just a lease, a licence, and a whole lot of "figure it out as you go."

The next question hit me like a freight train: *How do I avoid going bankrupt?*

The answer came fast: *Become the school they say I am. Teach. Enroll students. Earn enough to cover the lease.*

And the golden question followed close behind:

How do you actually *prove* you're a school?

That moment was the accidental beginning of a journey I never saw coming—one filled with audits, accreditations, government forms, success stories, failures, passion, grit, and more than a few breakdowns-turned-breakthroughs.

This book is my way of answering that golden question—for you.

The Truth: Anyone Can Teach… But Teaching Well—And Legally—is a Different Matter

If you've ever dreamed of teaching what you know, if you've found yourself mentoring others and thinking, *"I could turn this into something,"* or if—like me—you somehow stumbled into the role by accident… this is for you.

Because here's the truth:

Anyone can teach.

You don't need a university degree or a formal title to pass on knowledge. You don't need permission to help others grow. If you've lived it, practiced it, refined it—and your heart is in the right place—then yes, you can absolutely teach.

But teaching well… and teaching legally?

That's where most people get stuck.

It's not about perfection. It's about structure, responsibility, and clarity.
It's about understanding the difference between a *good idea* and a *functioning school.*

Running a course out of your living room might be legal—or it might not, depending on where you are. Issuing a certificate might be meaningful—or it might carry no weight if your students can't use it to get insurance or start a business. Calling yourself a school might be allowed—or it might require a business licence, city inspection, and clear curriculum outcomes.

And yet… none of this is meant to stop you.
It's meant to prepare you.

This book isn't about jumping through hoops. It's about giving you the roadmap I never had—the one that turns *"I think I want to teach"* into a sustainable, impactful school that changes lives (including your own).

So whether you're just exploring the idea or already knee-deep in lease agreements and lesson plans, let's make sure you build something you can be proud of—something that works, something that lasts, and something that aligns with your calling.

Because if I did it—with zero warning and no blueprint—you can too.

What Does It Really Mean to Be a Teacher?

And Where Do You Fit In?

When most people hear the word "teacher," they immediately think of someone standing in front of a chalkboard—certified, salaried, and working in a public school.

But in reality, "teacher" is a much broader and more inclusive term.

Let's break it down.

Early Childhood Educators (Preschool/Daycare)

- Teach children ages 0–5
- Often require certifications or diplomas in Early Childhood Education (ECE)
- Typically licensed through provincial/state education bodies

Primary & Secondary Teachers (K–12)

- Work in elementary, middle, and high schools
- Must be certified through a government-regulated education program
- Teach standardized curriculum
- Hired by public or private schools and follow ministry/state standards

Post-Secondary Teachers (College & University)

- Often called instructors, professors, or trainers
- May or may not have formal teaching degrees (especially in colleges and vocational schools)
- Hired based on experience + credentials in their field
- Teach adults or young adults in diploma, certificate, or degree programs

If you've taught at a college, private training institute, or adult learning center, you're considered a post-secondary educator.

Adult Educators, Private Trainers, and Workshop Leaders (That's You!)

This is the category most course creators, wellness professionals, coaches, and trainers fall into.

You may:

- Teach in your own studio, home, clinic, or rented classroom
- Offer certification or certificate programs in your own methods or modalities
- Create online courses for personal growth, business skills, holistic healing, beauty, etc.
- Work outside of government-run education—but still be held to professional standards

You are a teacher—just not in the traditional K–12 sense. You're a private adult educator, and you may even run your own school.

So… Can You Call Yourself a Teacher?

Yes, you can.
If you:

- Deliver structured lessons
- Support student learning
- Provide feedback and assessment
- Have a clearly defined subject or skill set you teach

…then you're a teacher.

You may not be certified by the Ministry of Education, but that doesn't make your role less real or valuable. In fact, many adult learners are seeking exactly what you offer—real-world experience, transformational learning, and flexible formats outside of traditional institutions.

Summary: Which Kind of Teacher Are You?

Type of Teacher	Requires Government Certification?	Teaches Children?	Teaches Adults?	Can Issue Certificates?
Preschool / ECE	Yes	Yes	No	Sometimes
K–12 School Teacher	Yes	Yes	No	No
College / University Instructor	Sometimes	No	Yes	Yes (institution-backed)
Private Adult Educator (You)	No	No	Yes	Yes

You don't need permission to teach—just structure, professionalism, and integrity.

This book will show you how to step into your role fully, legally, and with confidence.

What You'll Gain from This Book

This book is your real-world roadmap to turning your expertise into a recognized school, training program, or certification course—whether you're hosting a single weekend workshop or building a multi-year diploma program.

You'll learn how to:

- ## Turn your knowledge into a teachable, structured curriculum
  – Even if you've never taught before or written a single lesson plan.

- ## Understand what makes a school "legal" across jurisdictions
  – Including business licenses, zoning laws, fire inspections, teacher credentials, and post-secondary rules.

- ## Issue meaningful certificates and diplomas
  – So your students can get insurance, business licenses, and professional credibility—without overpromising.

- ## Navigate provincial, state, and national regulations
  – Know when you're exempt, when to register, and how to stay compliant in BC, Alberta, Ontario, the U.S., UK, Australia, and beyond.

- ## Design for transformation—not just information
  – Build courses that meet adult learner needs, support diverse learning styles, and leave lasting impact.

- ## Own your curriculum and protect your content
  – Avoid the costly mistake of licensing someone else's course without clear agreements.

- Avoid the biggest mistakes new school founders make
  – Like choosing the wrong name, opening without zoning approval, or getting sued over cross-border student files.
- Understand the difference between education, registration, and accreditation
  – And how each one impacts your school's reputation, legality, and longevity.
- Plan for growth—and protect your legacy
  – Whether you want to stay a one-person training center or scale into a team or franchise model.

By the end, you won't just feel inspired.

You'll have:

- A clear checklist of steps to follow
- Sample contracts, refund policies, and student recordkeeping standards
- Insight into audits, trust funds, instructor credentials, and naming laws
- And a full picture of what it really takes to turn your passion into a school—and your school into a legacy.

Let's begin.

Part 1: Your Knowledge Is Enough *(If You Structure It Right)*

Chapter 1: From Passion to Program

Who Can Teach Legally? (The Real Answer)

Let's begin with a question that stops many talented people in their tracks:

"Am I even allowed to teach this?"

Maybe you've worked in your field for years. Maybe people already come to you for advice. Maybe you've created your own method or unique approach—and you've started thinking, *Could I teach this? Could I offer a certificate? Could this be... a school?*

Here's the real answer:

Yes—you can teach. Legally.
No—you don't need a master's degree in education.
Anyone can teach. But the key is teaching with clarity, structure, and legal awareness.

You don't need a government-issued teaching degree to educate others in most private, non-accredited schools. Especially in unregulated industries—like coaching, energy work, spa services, wellness, creative arts, beauty, and personal development—there are few formal rules about *who* can teach.

The Misconception

A lot of people believe that you have to be certified by some higher authority or registered with a ministry to teach others—especially if you want to issue a certificate or diploma. But that's not true in most cases.

In most provinces, states, and countries:

- Anyone can teach a course.
- Anyone can offer a class, workshop, or seminar.
- Anyone can create and sell a program.

The difference is in the type of content you teach and the implied authority behind your certification.

If you're teaching something that is not regulated by law (like Reiki, business coaching, herbalism, reflexology, personal growth, or creative writing), you don't need government approval to teach it. You need a business licence (in most areas), professionalism, and clarity in how you present yourself.

All About the Post-Secondary Teacher's Diploma
What Is a Post-Secondary Teacher's Diploma?

A Post-Secondary Teacher's Diploma (also known in some provinces as an Instructor Diploma or Provincial Instructor Diploma) is a formal certification that qualifies an individual to teach adult learners in colleges, vocational schools, and private career training institutions. It focuses on adult education principles, curriculum development, classroom management, and effective teaching strategies for post-secondary students.

Who Needs One?

You may need a post-secondary teaching credential if:

- You want to teach in a government-accredited college or institution.
- Your province requires instructors to have formal teaching credentials in registered or accredited schools.
- You're applying for instructor approval from a governing body (like PTIB in BC) as part of a regulated program.
- You're looking to build credibility and trust as a course creator or school founder.

In many provinces, regulated schools must have at least one certified post-secondary teacher on staff to qualify for accreditation or registration.

When Should You Get It?

Best time to pursue it:

- When you're moving beyond hobby workshops to structured certificate/diploma programs.
- Before applying for school registration or accreditation.
- If you're planning to hire instructors and want to model professional standards.
- If your province's education board requires it for your teaching role approval.
- When you plan to scale or franchise your courses.

Even if you're a skilled practitioner, having this diploma shows your commitment to educational quality and compliance.

How to Get a Post-Secondary Teacher's Diploma

Each province offers its own version. Here's a general process:

Requirements:

- Work or education experience in the subject you want to teach.
- English fluency (often required for instruction and assignments).
- Usually, no degree is required, but a strong professional background is essential.

Programs (Examples):

- **British Columbia**: *Provincial Instructor Diploma Program (PIDP)* – offered by Vancouver Community College https://www.vcc.ca
- **Alberta**: *Adult Educator Certificate* or *Facilitator of Adult Learning* from NorQuest or similar colleges
- **Ontario**: *Adult Education* programs through community colleges or OISE (University of Toronto)
- **Online options**: Several Canadian institutions offer **remote learning** versions of these diplomas

Duration:

- 1–2 years part-time (flexible, often done while working)
- Some modules can be taken one at a time and completed at your own pace

What It Means for Your School

- Adds **credibility and professionalism** to your institution
- May be a **requirement for regulated training programs**
- Shows students and regulators you follow **recognized adult learning standards**
- Can help you **register as a qualified instructor** with PTIB or other governing bodies

Summary: Should You Get It?

You Should Get It If...	You Can Wait If...
You're planning to teach in a registered or accredited school	You're only running workshops under 40 hours/$4000
You're applying to be listed as an approved instructor	You're the sole teacher in a hobby-style course
You want to expand into multiple programs	You're testing a program concept before scaling
You're hiring staff and setting standards	You're just starting with informal classes

In regulated post-secondary institutions—such as those overseen by BC's PTIB or similar bodies—every instructor teaching career-focused or practical programs must be qualified. This typically means holding a relevant certificate, diploma, degree, or completing a Post-Secondary Teacher's Diploma—often called the Provincial Instructor Diploma Program (PIDP) in BC.

Instructor Qualification Requirements (BC Example – PTIB Rules)

1. Qualified Instructor Standard
   Every instructor teaching a career-related program must have:
     o A relevant certificate, diploma, or post-secondary degree plus 2 years of relevant work experience,
       or

- o 10 years of full-time work experience in their field.

2. Use of Substitutes

   Schools may use substitute instructors who do not meet these qualifications, but only for up to 10% of the program hours.

3. Senior-Educational Administrator (SEA)

   Accredited institutions must appoint an SEA—usually someone with a teaching diploma or equivalent—responsible for curriculum oversight and instructor performance reviews

Where the Post-Secondary Teacher's Diploma (PIDP) Fits In

- PIDP (Provincial Instructor Diploma Program) is a recognized credential across BC and other provinces.
- Offered via colleges like VCC, TRU, BCIT, lasting approximately 450 hours over ~10 months.
- Graduates are fully qualified to teach in private and public post-secondary institutions.
- PIDP can also fulfill the SEA requirement in accredited schools.

How Many Teachers Need It?

All instructors teaching practical or vocational courses in a regulated or accredited school must meet qualification standards. Though not *all* may require PIDP specifically, those teaching a significant portion of program hours typically do—especially in roles like SEA, or when the institution is scaling or seeking accreditation.

Summary Table

Role/Instructor Type	Qualification Requirement
All vocational/practical instructors	Diploma, degree + 2 years experience *or* 10 years on-the-job experience
Senior Educational Administrator (SEA)	Typically requires PIDP or equivalent credential
Substitute instructors	Qualifications waived *for up to 10% of program hours*

Bottom Line

- Every lead instructor in a registered or accredited school must be formally qualified.
- PIDP is the standard route to meet this requirement in BC (and often referenced elsewhere).
- SUBSTITUTE teachers may cover up to 10% of hours, but primary instructors should be fully credentialed.

Instructor Certification: Regulated vs. Unregulated Courses

1. Regulated Courses

These are programs that are monitored by a government or industry authority because they lead to a licensed or certified profession (e.g., Massage Therapy, Cosmetology, Esthetics, Electrician, Practical Nursing).

Instructor Requirements:

- Must meet minimum qualifications set by the governing body.
- Often need to hold a:
  - Teaching credential (like a Post-Secondary Instructor Diploma or Provincial Instructor Diploma Program—PIDP in BC)
  - License or certification in the field they're teaching
  - Minimum years of experience in practice
- Teaching without proper qualifications can result in fines, loss of school registration, or legal action.

Example:

To teach Massage Therapy in a regulated province like Ontario or BC, instructors may need:

- A valid RMT license
- 2–5 years of active practice
- Teaching credential (PIDP or equivalent)
- CPR/First Aid

2. Unregulated Courses

These are programs in fields not currently regulated by provincial/federal authorities, like:

- Reiki
- Reflexology
- Life Coaching
- Crystal Healing
- Energy Work
- Aromatherapy (depending on use)

Instructor Requirements:

- No government-set standards
- You set your own teaching standards unless you choose to affiliate with an association
- Best practice:
  - Have relevant experience and credentials
  - Provide a clear Instructor Certificate or Trainer Certificate
  - Include a teaching practicum, feedback process, and code of ethics

Important Consideration:

Even if unregulated, you still owe students a duty of care and should ensure your materials are safe, evidence-informed, and ethical.

Instructor Certificate: Should You Provide One?

Yes, especially for unregulated modalities.

Offer an Instructor Certificate when someone completes:

- Your core training +
- An additional "Train-the-Trainer" module that covers:
    - How to teach the content
    - Ethics
    - Client safety
    - Teaching methods and student engagement
    - Assessment and student tracking

This builds your brand's credibility and helps your modality grow into a recognized standard.

Summary Chart

Course Type	Regulated Course	Unregulated Course
Governed by	Government/Industry body (e.g., PTIB, Ministry)	No official regulator
Instructor must have	Field-specific license + teaching credential	Experience + optionally teaching certificate
Example Fields	RMT, Cosmetology, Hairstyling, Nursing	Reiki, Aromatherapy, Energy Healing
Association Affiliation	Often mandatory	Optional but recommended for credibility
Instructor Certificate	Not usually issued— regulated titles are sufficient	Highly recommended to set standards

Teacher Qualifications by Province/Territory

Jurisdiction	Regulated (Registered/Accredited) Programs — *PIDP or Equivalent Required?*	Unregulated (workshops / <40 hrs, <$4 k) — *PIDP Typically* Not Required
British Columbia	✅ Yes – PTIB requires instructors to have a teaching credential (degree, PIDP, or equivalent experience); PIDP often needed, especially for Senior Education Admin roles	❌ No – PIDP not required, though recommended for credibility
Alberta	✅ Likely – public/private colleges expect Adult Educator Certificate or PIDP; standard for vocational programs	❌ No – PIDP optional
Saskatchewan / Manitoba / Ontario	✅ Yes – vocational/private career colleges generally require teaching credentials or equivalent experience	❌ No – PIDP not mandatory

Jurisdiction	Regulated (Registered/Accredited) Programs — *PIDP or Equivalent Required?*	Unregulated (workshops / <40 hrs, <$4 k) — *PIDP Typically* Not Required
Other Territories (e.g. Yukon, NWT, Nunavut)	✅ Generally follow provincial standards, expect adult educator certification or equivalent credentials	❌ No – PIDP optional
Unregulated Programs (All Canada)	❌ No – short courses in unregulated fields (Reiki, reflexology, etc.) do *not* require PIDP or equivalent	✅ No – Instructor qualification set by school but not regulated

Notes & Clarifications

- In many provinces, PIDP (Provincial Instructor Diploma Program—e.g., BUVC, BCIT) is the recognized standard for teaching adults in regulated institutions.
- Industry experience alone (10+ years) or relevant degrees/certificates may substitute for PIDP in some jurisdictions.
- Unregulated courses, under thresholds like PTIB's 40 hours/$4k rule, do not legally require instructor diplomas—though they enhance credibility.

Summary

- Regulated programs (longer, vocational, accredited) require a teaching diploma or equivalent credential to ensure educational quality and compliance.
- Unregulated offerings (hobby-style, short courses) do not have such legal mandates, but professional standards still matter.

To Register Your Course/Program or Not

If your course always stays under 40 hours in length and under $4000 CAD in tuition, here's what that means:

You Do Not Need to Register with PTIB (or similar regulatory body)

This is because:

- In British Columbia (under the *Private Training Institutions Branch*, or PTIB), registration is only required if a program is:
  - More than 40 instructional hours, or
  - Costs more than $4000 CAD in total (including books, materials, etc.)

Most other provinces follow a similar guideline, though some use only one trigger or have slightly different thresholds.

You Can Still:

- Teach the course legally without registration.
- Issue a certificate of completion (not a diploma).
- Offer it in person, online, or hybrid.
- Promote it through your own school name (as long as the name complies with naming regulations—no misuse of "college," "university," etc.).

But You Still Need To:

1. Register Your Business (sole proprietor, partnership, or incorporation).
2. Get Proper Insurance (especially if hands-on).
3. Have a Clear Contract and Refund Policy.
4. Track Tuition and Expenses appropriately for tax and legal purposes.
5. Protect Your Intellectual Property (copyright your materials).

Important Limits:

Even if you're legally under the threshold:

- Students cannot get government loans or tax credits.
- You're not recognized as an official college or accredited institution.
- If you stack courses or offer "levels," PTIB or a similar agency may consider it one larger program and require registration.

Pro Tip:

If you plan to stay small, this is a great way to teach without red tape.
But if you're scaling, hiring instructors, or bundling modules—keep records and consider preparing for registration or accreditation when you grow.

When Regulation Comes Into Play

The moment you start teaching something that is governed by a regulatory body—like Massage Therapy, Esthetics, or anything in the medical or trade professions—you must follow the rules of that association or governing board.

This is where the word "school" can get tricky.

If you say you're a Massage School in a province where massage is a regulated profession, but you're not recognized by the provincial college or board? You can get into serious trouble. The same goes for teaching things like "Doctor-level" courses or calling your training "accredited" when it isn't.

That's why this book will walk you through:

- What you *can* legally say
- How to structure your teaching professionally
- When to get licensed or accredited
- How to avoid misrepresenting your courses—even by accident

The Heart of It All

Being a good teacher starts with one thing:
Knowing your stuff.

If you've spent years learning, practicing, and refining your knowledge… if people already come to you for advice… if you've helped others succeed, transform, or grow in some way—you're already teaching. This book will help you do it legally, confidently, and sustainably.

Quick Checklist: Can You Legally Teach Right Now?

If you answer yes to most of these, you're ready to begin:

- You have lived or professional experience in your subject.
- You are not claiming to grant a license to practice in a regulated field (unless authorized).
- You are honest about what your course offers.
- You are willing to register your business and follow local rules.

Owning Your Courses vs. Teaching Someone Else's

One of the biggest lessons I learned when my school became accredited was this:

If you don't own your curriculum, you don't control your school.

Owning Your Course Material

When you create and own the courses you teach, you:

- Have full rights to deliver, update, license, or protect your content.
- Can train other instructors without risking your entire program.
- Ensure continuity for students—even if a teacher leaves.
- Can seek accreditation, government registration, and insurance approval using *your name* and *your materials*.

This becomes especially important if:

- You want to scale your school with multiple teachers.
- You plan to franchise or license your programs.
- You want to ensure students receive what they paid for, regardless of instructor turnover.

When I became an accredited college, one of the requirements was that all course material must be owned by the institution, not an individual teacher. Why? Because students are enrolling in the *school*, not a person. If the instructor leaves—

and the course goes with them—students are left in limbo, and that opens the school up to legal, ethical, and regulatory issues.

Teaching Someone Else's Course (e.g., Reflexology from RAC)

Teaching a course licensed or created by another organization—such as RAC (Reflexology Association of Canada)—means:

- You must be certified through their process to teach under their brand.
- You must follow their curriculum and issue their certificates.
- You typically do not own or control the content.
- If your agreement ends or changes, you may lose the right to offer that course entirely.

This can be fine for solo educators or partnerships—but for a school model, it's risky unless you have clear licensing agreements in place that protect your operations long-term.

Accreditation Rules on Curriculum Ownership
1. Curriculum Must Belong to the Institution

Accredited schools must prove that they own or have licensed rights to all course content, including:

- Manuals
- Lesson plans
- Exams/quizzes
- Assignments
- Assessments
- Videos or teaching materials
- Student handouts and workbooks

This means:

- The school retains the course if a teacher leaves.
- Students will still get the training they paid for.
- The institution, not the individual teacher, is responsible for updating and maintaining quality.

2. Licensing Someone Else's Course? You Need Legal Rights

If your school uses a course developed by a third party (e.g., RAC Reflexology or another modality provider), you must have a formal licensing agreement with:

- Written permission to deliver the program.
- Clarity on ownership, updates, and assessment standards.
- Proof that the certifying body (e.g., RAC) allows your institution to teach under their standards.

Without this, your program may not be approved for accreditation.

3. Individual Instructor-Owned Curriculum Not Allowed (Without Transfer Agreement)

Accrediting agencies don't want a school to lose access to curriculum just because an instructor leaves. Therefore:

- If a course was developed by a contractor or teacher, the school must have the intellectual property (IP) rights or a course use contract.
- Ideally, teachers sign an assignment of rights or work-for-hire agreement stating that the curriculum belongs to the school.

4. Curriculum Submission for Accreditation

When applying for accreditation, you must submit:

- Course outline and learning objectives
- Assessment strategies
- Sample lessons or modules
- Any textbooks or third-party content with proof of rights

If you don't own or have licensed rights, the course will be rejected from the accreditation application.

What You Can Do:

- Write your own courses or hire curriculum developers under a contract that transfers ownership.
- Use open-source or public domain materials that are legally usable.

- If using someone else's curriculum, secure a non-expiring license with terms for accreditation use.

Final Thought:

Accreditation is not just about quality—it's about consistency and student protection. If you don't own the course, you can't guarantee delivery, and the accrediting body won't risk student tuition on that.

Best Practice

If you're serious about starting a school or becoming accredited, it's strongly advised to:

1. Create your own versions of the courses you're trained in (using your experience and additional research).
2. Write your own manuals, assessments, and certifications.
3. If you must teach someone else's material, negotiate written agreements outlining:
   - o Licensing rights
   - o Renewal terms
   - o What happens if the partnership ends
   - o Whether you're allowed to teach other similar content

Summary

Teaching Approach	Ownership	Control	Risk
Your Own Course	✓ Yes	✓ Full	✓ Low
Licensed Course	✗ No	⚠ Limited	⚠ Medium
No Agreement	✗ No	✗ None	✗ High

Step-by-Step Guide: Teacher to School Founder

Here's a step-by-step guide for someone who wants to go from *teacher* to *school founder*, starting with a single workshop and scaling to a full 4-year program:

PHASE 1: Start as a Teacher

Step 1: Master Your Craft

- Have a minimum of 1–2 years of experience practicing what you want to teach.
- Gather testimonials or case studies to validate your expertise.

Step 2: Create a Signature Workshop

- Teach a **single topic** in a 1-day or weekend format.
- Include:
    - Clear learning outcomes
    - Hands-on practice or guided exercises
    - Certificate of attendance (optional but helps with credibility)

Step 3: Legal Basics

- Register a **business name** and get a basic business license.
- Get **instructor liability insurance**.
- Ensure **zoning** allows for instruction (even if at home or online).

PHASE 2: Build Courses & Curriculum

Step 4: Turn Your Method into Teachable Modules

- Break your method into core components.
- Create lesson plans, videos, PDFs, and assignments.

Step 5: Develop a Certificate Course

- 20–60 hours total with evaluation (written or practical).
- Include:
  - Learning objectives
  - Intake & consent forms
  - Completion criteria (exam, case studies, final project)

Step 6: Register with an Association (Optional)

- This adds credibility and may help your students get insurance.
- Some associations offer course approval for CE credits.

PHASE 3: Found a School

Step 7: Choose a Name (Do It Right!)

- Search for existing trademarks and domain names.
- Avoid protected words like "College" or "University" unless permitted.

Step 8: Design a Program (over 40 hrs or $4000? Register!)

- 3–12 month foundational program
- Include multiple certificate courses as modules

- Ensure your curriculum includes:
  - Assessments
  - Outcomes
  - Structure
  - Contact & self-study hours

Step 9: Register with Your Province (if required)

- If in BC: PTIB (Private Training Institutions Branch)
- If in other provinces/states: check with your Ministry or Department of Education
- Accreditation is NOT the same as registration—choose based on your goals.

PHASE 4: Expand to 1–4 Year Programs

Step 10: Add Levels or Years

- Level 1 (Year 1) – Foundations (e.g., 400–1000 hrs)
- Level 2 – Intermediate (adds depth + specialized modalities)
- Level 3 – Advanced (complex clients, business ownership)
- Level 4 – Mastery (research, teaching skills, leadership)

Step 11: Consider Accreditation

- Optional, but helps if students want student loans, grants, or tax receipts.
- Requires audited records, instructor qualifications, and long-term commitment.

BONUS STEPS:

Step 12: Create Student & Instructor Handbooks

- Outline rules, code of conduct, grading, attendance, etc.

Step 13: Digital Record Keeping

- Use systems like Data Witness or secure cloud systems to store:
    o Student contracts
    o Transcripts
    o Certificates
    o Financial records (for at least 55 years in BC)

Step 14: Prepare for Audits

- Regularly review finances, refund policies, teacher credentials, and student outcomes.

Here's A Breakdown Of When To Incorporate, Register, Or Pursue Accreditation

based on stages from teacher to school founder:

PHASE 1: TEACHER STAGE (Workshop Level)

Business Registration

- **When:** As soon as you begin offering paid workshops or services.
- **Why:** Legal requirement for operating, even if teaching informally.
- **How:** Register your business name provincially (or federally, if you operate in multiple provinces/states).

Not Needed Yet:

- Incorporation
- Accreditation
- School registration

PHASE 2: COURSE CREATOR STAGE (Single or Multi-Module Courses)

Incorporation (Optional but Recommended)

- **When:** Once you begin offering more structured training, hiring contractors, or handling larger tuition.
- **Why:**
  - Protects your personal assets.
  - More professional when working with associations or offering certifications.
  - Easier to open a dedicated business bank account.

- How: Incorporate provincially (or federally if you operate across provinces or internationally).

Association Course Approval (Optional)

- When: If your students need professional recognition or insurance.
- Why: Helps legitimize your course and attract more serious students.
- Note: You don't have to be accredited to do this—but your curriculum must meet their standards.

PHASE 3: SCHOOL FOUNDER STAGE (Certificate or Diploma Program)

Private School Registration

- When: As soon as:
  - Your program exceeds 40 hours OR
  - Tuition exceeds $4000 CAD (in BC or similar provincial rules).
- Why: Required by law. Without registration, you're at risk of fines, shutdowns, or lawsuits—even if your school is home-based or online.

Incorporation (Must-Have by Now)

- Required for registered institutions.
- Must name your Directors and submit annual filings.

Accreditation (Still Optional)

- Only needed if:
  - You want students to access government loans/grants.
  - You want designated institution status.
  - You're scaling into multi-year diploma programs.

PHASE 4: FULL PROGRAM DEVELOPMENT (Multi-Year Diplomas)

Accreditation

- When: If you're offering 2–4 year programs or want to appear on par with public colleges.
- Why: Boosts credibility and allows students to claim education credits or loans.
- How: Apply through your province/state's higher education governing body (e.g., PTIB in BC).

RECAP BY STAGE

Stage	Incorporation	Registration	Accreditation
Workshop Only	✗ Optional	✓ Yes	✗ No
Single Certificate Course	✓ Recommended	✓ If over 40 hrs or $4K	✗ Optional
Multi-Course Program	✓ Required	✓ Required	✗ Optional
2–4 Year Program	✓ Required	✓ Required	✓ Optional (but strongly recommended)

Chapter 2: Who Owns the School?

Understanding Ownership Models: Sole Proprietor, Partnership, or Corporation

1. Sole Proprietorship

- Owned by one individual (you).
- Easiest and cheapest to set up.
- You are personally liable for everything—debts, lawsuits, audits.
- You operate under your own name or a registered business name (DBA).
- All school income is taxed as personal income.
- You own the curriculum, assets, and bank accounts directly.

Best for:

- Starting out with low risk
- Running small, home-based schools or short-term programs

Caution:

- **No legal separation** between you and your business—if someone sues the school, they're suing you personally.

2. Partnership

- **Two or more people** share ownership and responsibility.
- Informal unless a **legal agreement** is signed (highly recommended).
- Each partner is liable for the other's actions unless incorporated.
- All partners share profits, liabilities, and decision-making.

Best for:

- Co-founding with someone you trust (spouse, colleague)

Caution:

- Disagreements or one partner's mistake can affect the whole business.
- Ownership of the curriculum must be clearly defined.

3. Corporation (Incorporated School or College)

- The **corporation is its own legal entity**, separate from you.
- Owned by **shareholders**, managed by **directors**, and operated by **officers** (can be the same people in small schools).
- Can be for-profit or non-profit.

- The corporation owns all curriculum, assets, bank accounts, and contracts.
- Taxes are filed separately from your personal income.

Best for:

- Schools seeking accreditation, large enrollment, and liability protection
- Offering diplomas, hiring teachers, leasing/renting space

Consider:

- More paperwork (annual returns, director appointments, audits)
- Must follow strict governance rules (especially if applying for accreditation)

4. Non-Profit Society or Charity

- May operate a school under a registered nonprofit or charitable status.
- Owned by the organization, not any individual.
- Run by a board of directors, it must reinvest profits back into the mission.
- Eligible for grants and some tax exemptions.
- Still requires licensing and curriculum ownership.

Best for:

- Schools with a mission-based focus or funded by grants/donations
- Programs seeking long-term community impact

Accreditation & Legal Responsibilities by Ownership Type

Structure	Who Signs Agreements	Who's Sued if Something Goes Wrong	Who Owns Curriculum
Sole Proprietor	You personally	You personally	You or by contract
Partnership	One or all partners	All partners jointly	Must be agreed on
Corporation	Authorized director	The corporation (not personal)	The corporation
Non-Profit	Board of directors	The nonprofit organization	The nonprofit

Final Note:

If you plan to scale, incorporation offers more legal protection and credibility, especially for accreditation and insurance purposes.

However, starting as a sole proprietor can work if you're just testing the waters.

The Money: Who's Paying and For What?

Whether you're starting a small workshop-based school or building a full accredited college, understanding the financial flow is critical for sustainability—and legal compliance.

1. Startup Costs: Who Pays?

If you're the founder/owner, the startup costs usually come from:

- Your personal savings
- A business loan or line of credit
- Silent investors or partners
- Government grants (if eligible)

Typical startup expenses include:

- Business license and registration fees
- Lease deposit and rent
- Renovations (zoning/fire/ADA compliance if required)
- Equipment, desks, massage tables, facial beds, etc.
- Insurance (liability, contents, business interruption)
- Initial curriculum development or course rights
- Website and branding
- Legal fees (contracts, incorporation)
- First 3–6 months of operational overhead

Important:

If you don't track who paid for what (especially with partners or family), disputes can arise over who owns what and who is owed back if things go sideways.

2. Ongoing Expenses: What Does the School Pay For?

Once open, the school's business account should cover:

- Instructor salaries or contractor fees
- Rent, utilities, cleaning
- Insurance renewals
- Software (booking systems, learning platforms, data storage)
- Printing and student materials (manuals, handouts)
- Advertising & marketing
- Payments to government bodies (PTIB, annual reports, etc.)

All income from tuition must go through the school's official bank account—never through your personal account. This is especially important if you're regulated or accredited.

3. Student Tuition: What Are They Paying For?

Students believe they're paying for:

- Legitimate training that leads to opportunity
- A recognized certificate or diploma
- A structured experience that includes:
    - Manuals/workbooks
    - Classes (in person, hybrid, or online)
    - Assignments and exams
    - Teacher feedback
    - Access to support

You must clearly define in your enrollment contract:

- What the course includes
- Tuition total and breakdown (including taxes, if applicable)
- Any optional or mandatory supplies/kits
- Payment plan terms
- Refund policy (required by most regulatory bodies)

4. Who Holds the Money?

If incorporated:

- The corporation owns the income and expenses, not you personally.

If a sole proprietor:

- You are the business, but you should still have a separate business bank account.

If working with co-instructors:

- Ensure written agreements clarify:
  - How revenue is split
  - Who covers expenses
  - Who pays for marketing
  - Ownership of curriculum and students

5. Refunds, Audits & Legal Compliance

If you're offering courses over 40 hours or $4,000 (in BC), and you are not exempt, you must:

- Register with PTIB

- Hold tuition in trust until earned
- Offer refunds based on a regulated formula

Failure to do this can trigger audits, fines, or even lawsuits.

6. Paying Teachers or Guest Instructors

You may pay them as:

- Employees (T4 or payroll)
- Contractors (invoice you, no benefits, T4A or 1099 in U.S.)
- Revenue share (e.g., 30% of tuition)

You must clearly outline:

- Who owns the curriculum
- Who's responsible if the student complains or wants a refund
- Payment frequency and method
- If they must bring their own insurance

Final Tip:

Separate business and personal funds from day one.

It will protect you legally, simplify taxes, and keep you organized—especially if you plan to scale, get accredited, or bring in partners.

Personal vs. Business Bank Accounts

Whether you are just starting, already running a small course, or growing into an accredited school, here's why you must use a business bank account:

Why You Need a Business Bank Account

1. ## Legal Separation
   Using a personal account blurs the line between you and the business. If someone sues the school, you (personally) can be held liable.

2. ## Student Tuition Must Be Trackable
   If audited (especially by PTIB or another regulator), you must show:
   - Exactly when and how tuition was received
   - Whether the tuition was *earned* (i.e., the service was delivered)
   - That the funds were held and managed appropriately

3. ## Refunds and Trust Funds
   In most regulated provinces (like BC), student tuition must be held in trust until it's considered earned (based on class time delivered).
   A business bank account ensures:
   - Refunds are traceable
   - Government requirements are met
   - Student trust is protected

4. ## Professionalism and Tax Compliance
   - You can't deduct expenses or properly track GST/HST if it's all flowing through your personal account.
   - CRA can deny deductions or flag your returns.

If the School Closes

Depending on your business structure, here's what happens:

1. Sole Proprietor

- You are the school, legally.
- If the school closes and you've used your personal bank account, all school liabilities (refunds, lawsuits, etc.) come back to you personally.
- No student records or funds should be destroyed without notifying the governing body (e.g., PTIB).

2. Incorporated

- The business is a separate legal entity.
- Funds must go through the corporate bank account.
- Directors (you and/or others) are liable only in certain situations (e.g., fraud, mismanagement).
- You must file a dissolution notice and keep records for 7–55 years, depending on provincial law.

3. Accredited School

- You must comply with much stricter rules:
  - Student tuition must be held in trust until earned.
  - Clear refund timelines must be followed.
  - Student records must be held (often 55 years, either in-house or via approved digital custodians like DataWitness).
  - If you close, you must notify the accrediting body, and they must approve the teach-out plan or transition.

Changing Structures (Sole Proprietor → Incorporated → Accredited)

If you're shifting between these stages:

- Open a **new business bank account** aligned with the new entity.
- Transfer any existing obligations, contracts, or student tuition to the new structure **with legal documentation**.
- Notify your students and regulatory bodies of the change.
- Update any contracts, refund policies, or insurance coverage to reflect the new business name and entity.

Summary: DO NOT Use a Personal Account

- Even for one student, the moment you accept money for education, you are stepping into **regulated territory**.
- Protect yourself, your students, and your future.
- **Open a separate business bank account** early—even as a sole proprietor—and keep everything clean.

Holding Tuition in Trust Until Earned

This is one of the most important (and often misunderstood) financial rules when running a regulated or accredited school. Here's what it means to "hold tuition in trust until earned," why it matters, and how to stay compliant.

What It Means

If your school is registered or accredited under a regulatory body (like PTIB in BC), you are not allowed to treat all student tuition as "yours" the moment it's paid.

Instead, you must:

- Place the money into a designated trust account
- Only "draw down" the money as the student progresses through the program

This is a student protection rule—designed to ensure that if your school closes, the student can be refunded for unused training.

Example Breakdown

Let's say your student pays $6,000 for a 12-week course.

You must only move money from the trust account to your business operating account as the course is delivered. So:

- Week 1 = $500 earned
- Week 2 = another $500

- And so on…

If the student withdraws in Week 4, you've "earned" $2,000. The remaining $4,000 stays in trust and must be refunded according to your **refund policy** (which is usually set by law).

Why This Matters

If you **spend unearned tuition early** and a student withdraws (or PTIB audits you), you may:

- Be forced to pay **thousands in refunds**
- **Lose your accreditation or registration**
- Face **legal or financial penalties**
- Be blacklisted from future regulatory approval

How to Do It Properly

1. **Open two separate bank accounts:**
   - **Trust Account:** Holds prepaid tuition.
   - **Operating Account:** Where you transfer earned funds for expenses.
2. **Track each student's tuition timeline:**
   - How much they've paid
   - How much of the course have they completed
   - How much has been earned
3. **Follow your refund policy and update it annually.**
   - Use templates from your regulatory body (e.g., PTIB)
4. **Hire an accountant familiar with education regulations.**

   o   Many small schools get caught in audits due to
       mismanagement or lack of clarity.

Pro Tip:

Some schools use **tuition management software** or a
spreadsheet ledger to monitor tuition held in trust. You
should always be able to show, at any point:

- How much is in trust
- For which students
- For how much longer

Contracts, Refund Rules & When Tuition Becomes the School's

When a student enrolls in a course or program, a legally binding contract is created — even if it's not written in legalese. This contract outlines:

- What the student will receive (education, materials, credentials)
- What the student must do (attend, pay, complete assignments)
- What the school promises in return

If your school is registered with a provincial, state, or national regulatory body (such as PTIB in BC), then you are legally required to follow very specific rules about student contracts and refunds.

The Student Enrolment Contract Must Include:

1. Full course title and description
2. Start and end dates
3. Total hours or learning outcomes
4. Tuition cost and breakdown of fees (e.g., books, registration)
5. Refund policy
6. Payment schedule
7. Student responsibilities
8. School responsibilities
9. Cancellation clause and withdrawal process

Most regulatory bodies require a signed copy from both student and school, and it must be stored in the student file for 55 years.

How Refund Rules Work (General Guidelines)

These vary by province/state, but commonly follow this logic:

- ## Before the course begins:
  - Full refund minus admin/registration fee (if allowed)
- ## Up to 10% of course completed:
  - 70–90% refund of tuition
- ## 10%–30% of course completed:
  - 50–70% refund of tuition
- ## Over 30% completed:
  - No refund required; tuition is considered earned

Important: You cannot create your own refund rules if you're regulated — you must use the ones set by your governing body.

When Does the Tuition Become Yours (Earned)?

Tuition is only legally earned once the corresponding portion of training is delivered. This means:

- If a student drops out midway, you cannot keep 100% of their tuition unless your program is more than 30% complete.
- You must calculate the portion delivered and refund the rest from the trust account.

Illegal or Risky Practices to Avoid

- Taking full payment without a contract
- Not issuing receipts or tracking installments
- Spending tuition before it's earned (see "trust account" section)
- Failing to return unused fees when a student withdraws

Best Practices for Educators

- Always give students a **written and signed contract** before payment
- Make sure your **refund policy is crystal clear**
- Follow your governing body's **exact refund formulas**
- Communicate policies clearly during enrollment — transparency builds trust
- Store all contracts, payment logs, and correspondence in the student's permanent file

Refund Rules by Delivery Format

1. In-Person Learning

- Follow **standard refund rules** of your provincial/state regulatory body.
- Tuition is generally **held in trust** and only released to the school as the training progresses.
- If the student drops out early, **a pro-rated refund** is required.
- If your school is **PTIB-regulated (BC)** or similar, specific refund percentages are enforced by law.

2. Hybrid (In-Person + Online)

- Treated the same as in-person unless:
  - The online component is less than 10%, in which case it might be considered "supplemental."
  - Or if the student resides in another province/state, triggering cross-jurisdiction compliance issues.
- Refunds follow the same pro-rated structure based on participation or days completed.

3. Distance Education / Online

- If regulated (e.g., the course is vocational, over 40 hours or $4,000 in BC), the same refund laws apply.
- The student's progress (e.g., modules accessed or completed) determines how much tuition is "earned."
- If a student logs in but doesn't engage, you may still owe a refund.
- If you're offering online courses to students in other provinces/countries, you may be required to:
  - Register in their jurisdiction, or
  - Add disclaimers saying "this training is not intended for licensure in [province]" (if unregulated).

Important Notes

- Even if your program is delivered online, once a student pays and signs a contract, refund laws still apply.
- Most jurisdictions don't let schools say "no refunds" — even for digital access — unless clearly exempt or fully delivered.

- If your course is exempt (like a short hobby class or under 40 hours), you must still declare it as exempt when asked.

Best Practices

- Treat all delivery types with equal refund structure unless truly exempt.
- Log when students access content (for online) to justify earned tuition.
- Use clear refund clauses in your enrollment contracts, tailored by delivery format if needed.
- If in doubt, consult your provincial/state regulator or legal counsel — fines for non-compliance are steep.

How Time Affects Refunds in Regulated Programs

1. In-Person & Hybrid Programs

- "Days in class" refers to scheduled instructional days (e.g., Mon–Fri, 9am–3pm).
- Refunds are based on:
    - The number of calendar days between the student's start date and their withdrawal or dismissal, regardless of whether they attended every class.
- PTIB (BC) and similar regulators usually break this down into:
    - 0%–10% of program completed = high refund
    - 11%–30% = partial refund

o Over 30% = no refund

2. Distance Education (Online or Self-Paced)

- Time is calculated from the student's contract start date, not based on access or progress.
- Even if a student never logs in, the refund countdown begins on their start date (usually the contract signing or designated program start).
- Refund tiers still apply based on:
  o Calendar days elapsed between start and withdrawal/dismissal.
  o NOT how far into the material the student is.
- If your program has a set completion time (e.g., 6 months), the refund is pro-rated based on how many days into that timeframe they are when they leave.

Example: Distance Learning Refund Period

Let's say:

- Your online course is 180 days (6 months).
- A student enrolls and signs the contract on Jan 1.
- They ask for a refund on Jan 20.

Even if they only logged in once or not at all, 20 days have passed, so they've used ~11% of the course time.

Under PTIB:

- You would owe a partial refund, based on the table provided in their policy manual.

Refund Tied to "Time Allowed" to Complete, Not Actual Access

Format	Refund Based On...
In-Person	Calendar days between the first class and withdrawal
Hybrid	Same as in-person
Distance Ed	Calendar days from start date to withdrawal, not login

Best Practices

- Clearly state the course start date in your student contracts.
- Include the maximum duration allowed to complete the course.
- Track when students first access content — not for refund law, but to protect yourself if challenged.
- Ensure refund calculations align with provincial/state rules.

Example of the refund rules (BC), *check your province/state rules*

https://www.privatetraininginstitutions.gov.bc.ca/quality-standards

All forms
https://www.privatetraininginstitutions.gov.bc.ca/index.php/form-library

Then check out Tuition Refund Policy – Approved Program Sample (DOCX)

In Summary

Tuition isn't considered *earned* income until it aligns with legally or contractually defined milestones—such as time completed, content delivered, or progress made. For regulated schools, strict refund policies ensure accountability and protect students. For unregulated or private schools, your reputation, transparency, and clearly written contracts are your safeguard.

Whether you're running a government-certified college or a passion-based teaching practice from home, how and when you handle tuition reflects your professionalism—and can determine whether your school grows, gets audited, or shuts down. Treat tuition with care, clarity, and compliance, and you'll build both student trust and a sustainable business.

Student Loans & Refunds: Who Gets the Money?

When a student secures a loan (government or private) to pay for their course or program, the tuition payment often goes directly to the school. But if the student withdraws or is dismissed, things get more complex—and legally specific.

Refunds Must Go Back to the Loan Source

In most jurisdictions (especially under regulated bodies like PTIB or government student aid programs):

- The school must refund the unearned portion of tuition back to the lender, not the student.
- This includes:
  - StudentAid BC, Alberta Student Aid, OSAP, and other provincial or federal student loan programs.
  - Private lenders that require refund clauses in school contracts.

If a refund is issued directly to the student instead of the lender, and that student defaults, the school may be held liable for that money.

What the School Must Do:

- Maintain accurate records of attendance, progress, and withdrawal dates.
- Report withdrawals or changes in enrollment to the loan provider.
- Follow refund timelines set by the regulator or loan agreement.

- Issue the refund to the original payee—in this case, the loan provider—not the student.

In Summary:

If a student's tuition is funded through a loan, any applicable refund must go to the lender—not the student. This protects all parties and ensures financial integrity. Failure to do so can result in legal action, funding ineligibility, or loss of accreditation for the school.

Clear contracts, good bookkeeping, and open communication with both students and lenders are key to staying compliant and protecting your school's future.

Intake Forms, Consent Forms & Communication

Even If You Are Nonregulated

Start Smart, Protect Yourself, and Build Trust from Day One

You've put so much energy into creating your course, shaping your content, and structuring the learning journey. But before your student even watches the first video or walks through the door, there's one thing that matters just as much as your teaching:

The way you onboard them.

A well-prepared intake process builds confidence, sets expectations, and protects both you and your student from confusion or conflict later on. It shows that you're not just a passionate teacher—you're also a professional.

1. Intake Forms: More Than Just Paperwork

An intake form is your **first official interaction** with a student. It collects important information and gives your school a record of who enrolled, when, and what they agreed to.

Your intake form should include:

- Full legal name and contact info
- Emergency contact
- Relevant health disclosures (especially for bodywork or hands-on training)
- Course name and start date
- Payment terms (if applicable)
- Space for a student signature and date

Why it matters:

- It protects your business legally
- It's required for insurance and audits
- It reinforces boundaries and expectations

2. Consent Forms: Clarity Is Kindness

If your course includes:

- Touch-based techniques (massage, reflexology, facials, energy work)
- Case study exchanges
- Demonstrations on or by students

...you must have written consent.

Your consent form should clearly outline:

- What activities are included in the course
- Whether students will be giving/receiving treatments
- If they'll be photographed or recorded for assessment
- Their right to decline participation at any point

Make sure your language is plain, respectful, and unambiguous. A good consent form doesn't scare people—it informs them and gives them agency.

3. Communication: Set the Tone Early

Before the course even begins, send a Welcome Email or Orientation Packet that covers:

- What to expect (format, timing, structure)
- What to bring or prepare

- How to contact you with questions
- Policies around attendance, late work, or cancellations
- A link to download or digitally sign the intake & consent forms

If your course is in person, have printed copies ready on Day 1. If it's online, use a simple e-signature tool or PDF fillable forms.

Bonus: Keep Student Records Secure

Store all signed forms, assessments, and certificates in a secure digital folder or course management system. If you're ever audited, sued, or asked for proof of training by an association, this will be your saving grace.

Use:

- Google Drive (with folders by course/year)
- Dropbox or iCloud
- Course platforms like Thinkific, Teachable, or LearnDash

Final Checklist: What to Include in Your Intake Package

Form/Document	Purpose
Intake Form	Student identity and registration
Consent Form	Legal and ethical boundaries
Course Overview or Syllabus	Helps manage expectations
Terms & Policies Agreement	Attendance, refunds, behavior guidelines
Media Release (optional)	If using student photos or testimonials

Final Word:

Professionalism doesn't start in the classroom—it starts with the first form.

A strong intake and consent process:

- Builds student trust
- Protects your business
- Positions you as a credible school or training provider

It's one of the most powerful ways to shift from *"I teach a course"* to *"I run a school."*

Chapter 3: Course Creation Basics

Turning Your Method Into Teachable Modules

So you've got a skill, a system, or a way of doing things that gets results.
Maybe it's something you've refined through years of practice, or maybe you've developed your own unique method that others constantly ask you to teach.

That's your *gold*. Now it's time to turn it into a structure other people can follow.

Step 1: Start with the Transformation

Before you think about hours, handouts, or fancy course titles, ask yourself:

What will my students be able to do after this course that they couldn't do before?

That's your transformation. It's the real reason someone signs up—not just for *information*, but for a result.

Examples:

- In a reflexology course, *"Students will be able to confidently perform a 30-minute foot reflexology session."*

- In a Reiki program: *"Students will be attuned to Level I Reiki and understand how to use it for self-healing and others."*
- In a brow design workshop: *"Students will know how to map, shape, and style brows for various face shapes using both tweezing and tinting methods."*

Write this first. Then build everything else around it.

Step 2: Break It Into Logical Steps

Now take that transformation and ask:
What would someone need to learn, step by step, to reach that result?

These become your modules.

Example (for a beginner energy healing course):

1. Introduction to Energy Healing
2. Understanding the Chakras
3. How Energy Moves Through the Body
4. Learning the Hand Positions
5. Conducting a Self-Treatment
6. Practicing on Others Safely and Ethically
7. Closing Rituals and Grounding
8. Final Practice & Evaluation

Each module focuses on one concept or skill.
Keep them clear. Keep them sequential. And always ask:

"If I were learning this for the first time, what would I need to understand before moving to the next part?"

Step 3: Decide on Delivery

Not all modules need to be long. Not everything has to be written.
Think about *how* your students will best receive the information.

You can mix and match:

- Written PDFs (manuals, worksheets, checklists)
- Live or recorded videos
- Hands-on assignments or practice logs
- Quizzes or self-reflection questions
- Demonstration videos
- Live workshops or practicums (in person or online)

Hint: Adult learners love practical tools and clear instructions. Keep the fluff to a minimum and focus on what helps them succeed.

Step 4: Add Your Signature Touch

This is where your *method* shines.

Don't just teach what everyone else teaches. Show them *your* way of doing it:

- Your scripts
- Your forms
- Your client process
- Your stories
- Your tools
- Your do's and don'ts

This is how you stand out—and how your students will feel confident saying,

"I trained with [Your Name]. I learned the [Your Method Name] way."

Final Thought for This Section:

If you can teach someone one-on-one, you can turn it into a course.

If you can walk someone through a process out loud, you can structure it into modules.

If you've ever explained something and seen that "lightbulb moment," you've already started teaching.

Now we're just giving it form.

The 3 Pillars of a Good Course: Learning Outcomes, Assessment, Structure

Creating a course isn't just about sharing what you know—it's about guiding someone else through a clear, purposeful learning journey.

If you want to create a course that feels professional, delivers real value, and builds your credibility as a teacher or school, then these are the three pillars you must have in place:

Pillar 1: Learning Outcomes – The Destination

A *learning outcome* tells your student where they're going. It describes what they'll be able to know, do, or feel confident about after completing your course or module.

Each course should have:

- A main overall outcome (the transformation)
- Smaller module-specific outcomes (what they'll gain at each step)

Example – For a Crystal Healing Course:

- Course Outcome: Students will be able to identify, cleanse, and use crystals for energetic healing sessions.
- Module Outcome (for Module 2): Students will be able to classify common crystals by type and healing property.

Tip: Use action verbs like:

- "Identify"
- "Demonstrate"
- "Perform"
- "Apply"
- "Describe"
- "Create"

Avoid vague terms like "understand" or "know" when possible.

Pillar 2: Assessment – Proof of Learning

If outcomes are the destination, assessments are how you know they arrived.

Assessments don't have to be formal tests (unless your course requires it).
They can be:

- Case studies
- Written reflections
- Video submissions
- Demonstrations
- Short quizzes
- Before/after comparisons
- Peer feedback or instructor evaluations

You simply need to show:

"Yes, they learned what I said they would."

This is also important if your students need proof of competency for insurance, licensing, or professional association acceptance. Having some form of documented assessment shows that you didn't just hand out certificates—you taught and evaluated.

Pillar 3: Structure – The Framework That Holds It All Together

Think of structure like the scaffolding that supports the entire learning process.

A good structure includes:

- A clear course flow (intro → lesson → practice → review → next)
- Consistency in formatting (all modules look/feel the same)
- Defined duration (ex. 8 hours, 4 weeks, 30-day challenge)
- Accessible delivery (online portal, printed manual, in-person classroom)

Your structure should answer the student's unspoken question:

"How do I move through this course and know I'm on track?"

You can build a structure using:

- Welcome sections and orientation checklists
- Progress trackers or module checkboxes
- Consistent layout of lesson materials
- Clear milestones (e.g., "By the end of Module 3, submit your case study")

Consistency builds trust.
It makes your course feel professional—even if you're just starting out.

In Summary:

A good course doesn't need to be complicated—but it does need to be clear.
With these three pillars, you're not just teaching—you're

delivering a transformation that's repeatable, certifiable, and respected.

- Outcomes show the purpose.
- Assessment shows the proof.
- Structure shows the path.

Hours-Based vs. Outcome-Based Learning

When you begin creating your course—or your entire school—you'll quickly face an important decision:

Should my course be based on a required number of hours... or based on learning outcomes?

Both models are valid, but they serve different purposes. Understanding the difference helps you design smarter, teach more effectively, and avoid unnecessary roadblocks—especially if you plan to apply for accreditation, work with associations, or issue certificates that students use for insurance or licensing.

What Is Hours-Based Learning?

This is the traditional model. Many government-regulated schools and professional associations require a minimum number of instructional hours for a course or program to be accepted.

Examples:

- 700 hours for Massage Therapy certification (in some provinces)
- 300 hours for Esthetics
- 100 hours for Yoga Teacher Training
- 20 hours for a First Aid instructor course

With this model, the focus is:

- How many in-class or guided hours the student receives
- How many practice hours they complete (sometimes called "clinic" or "practicum")
- Less emphasis is placed on what the student can actually *do* by the end

When to Use Hours-Based:

- If your course is governed by a licensing body
- If you're trying to match industry standards
- If your students need specific hours for insurance coverage or association membership

What Is Outcome-Based Learning?

In this model, the emphasis is on what the student can do at the end of the course—regardless of how many hours it took to get there.

It's not about the time—it's about the transformation.

You design your program by asking:

- What are the skills or knowledge students must demonstrate?
- What assignments, case studies, or evaluations will show they've learned it?
- How will I support them in getting to that result?

With outcome-based learning:

- Students might move at different paces
- Courses can be shorter or longer, depending on the material
- Your certificate reflects competency, not just attendance

When to Use Outcome-Based:

- If you're teaching skills that aren't regulated by law
- If your focus is on personal growth, coaching, wellness, or energetic healing
- If your students are more interested in transformation than credentials
- If your goal is to certify based on skill, not time spent

Can You Combine Both?

Yes—and many successful private schools do.

For example, you can:

- Design a 20-hour program with clear outcomes and a final evaluation
- Include a minimum number of practice hours (for student accountability)
- Clearly state the time and the skills the student will gain

This hybrid model works especially well if:

- You want your certificate to be recognized by an association
- You want to balance structure with flexibility

- You eventually want to move toward accreditation or licensure pathways

Real Talk: What Matters Most?

A certificate with 100 hours means nothing if the student can't do the work.
A 5-hour course can change a life—if it's built on outcomes.

When it comes to building your school or course, the question isn't just *how long it is*.
It's:

"Does this course deliver what it promises?"
"Can the student actually apply what they've learned?"

That's what builds your reputation—and your business.

Online Platform & EdTech Tools: Choosing the Right System for Your School

If you're offering hybrid or online training, your learning platform is just as important as your curriculum. Choosing the wrong system—or skipping due diligence—can lead to technical breakdowns, privacy violations, and frustrated students. Let's explore what you need to know.

1. Recommended Online Course Platforms

These all-in-one platforms allow you to upload lessons, accept payments, track student progress, and even automate certificates. Here are the most commonly used systems in the industry:

Platform	Best For	Notable Features
Teachable	Beginners & solopreneurs	Drag-and-drop builder, built-in payment gateway
Thinkific	Growing schools & academies	White-label options, quizzes, certifications
Kajabi	Business owners needing full marketing	Funnels, email, automation, community features
Moodle	Larger or regulated institutions	Open-source, highly customizable, widely used
Podia	Digital product creators & coaches	Great for memberships and live webinars

Tip: If you're applying for *accreditation* or want tight student tracking, Moodle or Thinkific (Pro plans) are better suited for compliance and reporting.

2. LMS vs. Self-Hosted vs. Hybrid: Which One Should You Choose?

There's no one-size-fits-all answer. It depends on your school's goals, tech ability, and budget.

Option	Pros	Cons
LMS (Learning Management System)	Easy to set up, built-in features, support	Monthly fees, limited customization
Self-Hosted (e.g., LearnDash on WordPress)	Total control, no platform fees	Tech-heavy, you manage updates/security
Hybrid (Zoom + Dropbox + Manual Tracking)	Cost-effective for small programs	Harder to scale or meet compliance standards

If your school is **unregulated and just starting,** LMS platforms are faster to launch and less risky.

3. Data Residency: Where Are Your Student Records Stored?

This is **critical** if your school is regulated or intends to be. Many privacy and education laws (like PIPEDA in Canada or FERPA in the U.S.) require that student data be stored securely—and in many cases, on servers within your country.

Questions to ask your platform provider:

- Where are your servers located?
- Is data encrypted at rest and in transit?
- Do you offer Canadian server options (if operating in Canada)?
- Can I download and back up student data locally?

CA Canadian Requirement: Regulated institutions in Canada may need to prove that student records are stored in Canada or on a compliant server.

4. What to Look for in a Platform

Before you commit, make sure your platform offers:

- Student progress tracking
- Automated certificates
- Secure login with privacy tools
- Easy navigation for all tech levels
- Scalability for multiple programs or instructors
- Downloadable/exportable records for audits

Final Thoughts

Your platform is more than a tech tool—it's your classroom, registrar, and security system rolled into one. Choose a system that grows with you, protects your data, and keeps your students engaged and on track.

PDFs, Videos, Assignments – How Much Is Enough?

Creating Course Content That's Valuable, Not Overwhelming

One of the most common questions new course creators ask is:

"How much content do I actually need to include?"

The truth?
There's no one-size-fits-all answer—but there is a sweet spot between "just enough to teach well" and "so much that students get overwhelmed or disengaged."

Let's break it down.

PDFs – The Core of Your Written Content

PDFs are your foundational tools.
They can be:

- Course manuals
- Step-by-step instructions
- Diagrams or charts
- Intake or consent forms
- Checklists and reflection sheets

Best Practice:

- Include one main manual or workbook per course

- Supplement with short PDFs for complex modules (no more than 3–5 pages per add-on)
- Keep formatting clean, with headings, bullet points, and space to write if it's printable

Remember: Adult learners love handouts that are practical, printable, and to the point.

Videos – Visual Learning That Brings You to Life

Videos help students feel connected to you—and are essential for demonstrating techniques, especially in hands-on fields like esthetics, bodywork, or energy healing.

You can record:

- Welcome/introduction messages
- Technique demonstrations
- Module walk-throughs
- Guided meditations or visualizations
- Instructor tips or story-based videos

Best Practice:

- Keep videos short and focused: 5–15 minutes each
- Break big topics into bite-sized clips (rather than one long video)
- Use a mix of talking-head (you on camera) and screen shares or demos

You don't need fancy equipment. Clear sound, good lighting, and authenticity matter more than cinematic quality.

Assignments – Turn Learning Into Practice

Assignments (or practice activities) are where transformation happens.
Without them, your course becomes passive learning—information in, but no action out.

Assignments can include:

- Case studies
- Quizzes
- Journaling prompts
- Practice logs
- Worksheets
- Demonstration videos (for student submissions)

Best Practice:

- Include one practical assignment per module, even if small
- Make sure each one links back to a learning outcome
- Give clear instructions and an optional way to submit or track

Example:

In a Brow Design course, your Module 2 assignment might be:

"Map and measure 3 brows on paper using the golden ratio method. Submit a photo with your measurement notes."

This reinforces what they've learned and gives you a way to assess progress.

So... How Much Is Enough?

Here's a simple rule of thumb:

Content Type	Minimum	Ideal Range
PDFs (manuals/handouts)	1 main guide + 1 per module if needed	10–30 pages total
Videos	1 intro + 1 per module	5–15 min each, up to 1 hour total
Assignments	1 per module	5–8 thoughtful activities across the course

Your goal is not to flood the student with material.

Your goal is to guide them through a journey—clearly, confidently, and efficiently.

Final Thought:

Enough is when your student can succeed—without confusion.

Not more. Not less.

You're not trying to prove how much you know. You're creating a path for someone else to rise.

And with just the right amount of support, structure, and content—they will.

Certification vs. Education: What's the Difference—and Where Does Your Course Fit?

This is one of the most misunderstood topics in course creation, and it's also one of the most important.

People often use the words education, certification, certificate, and diploma interchangeably—but they don't all mean the same thing, especially in the eyes of government, insurance providers, or professional associations.

Knowing which one your course actually offers protects you, your students, and your reputation.

Education: Teaching Knowledge and Skills

Education is the act of transferring knowledge, skills, or insight to another person.
It doesn't require government approval.
It doesn't require an official stamp.
It requires that you know what you're teaching and that you deliver it in a clear, structured way.

If you:

- Teach someone a healing technique
- Offer a workshop on mindset coaching
- Run a course on business branding
- Show a student how to use tuning forks, reflexology, or Reiki

…you're providing education.

And guess what? That's completely legal in most jurisdictions—as long as you're not claiming that your course qualifies them for a *regulated* profession (like nurse, doctor, or lawyer).

Certification: Verifying a Standard Has Been Met

Certification is a form of validation that a student has achieved a set standard in a specific method, modality, or profession.

When you "certify" someone, you are saying:

"This person has completed my training and met the requirements I've laid out. I, as the authority, approve them to use my method or approach."

This is common in:

- Energy medicine
- Coaching
- Alternative health practices
- Artistic or entrepreneurial techniques

BUT:

Certification is only as meaningful as the credibility of the certifier.

If your name, your brand, or your school has a good reputation, your certification holds weight—especially if your students can use it to get insurance, work with clients, or join an association.

If you don't clarify what your certification means or how it can be used, you risk misleading students—even accidentally.

What You Need to Clarify

When creating your course, ask:

1. Is this education only, or am I certifying a skill set?
2. Can students use this to practice professionally?
3. Does my certification hold any external recognition—or am I creating my own standard?
4. Will this allow students to apply for insurance or register with a professional body?

Your answer determines how you market your course—and how you word your certificates.

Examples of Language to Use:

- *Certificate of Completion:*
  "This confirms participation in the [Course Name] program and acknowledges [Student Name] has completed the required training hours."
- *Certification Statement:*
  "This certifies that [Student Name] has successfully completed the requirements of [Your School/Method Name] and is approved to offer [Modality] services under the [Your Name] method."
- Avoid Saying:
  "Licensed practitioner" or "Registered Therapist" unless your course is approved by the governing body for that profession in your region.

How Your Course Can Fit Both

You can absolutely create a course that provides education and certification—if you clearly define:

- What your certification means
- What students can and cannot legally do with it
- What standards or assessments you've included to verify competence

When in doubt, be transparent.

Clarity protects you and empowers your students.

Final Word for This Section:

Education is about sharing what you know. Certification is about vouching for what someone else can do.

Both are valuable.
Both are powerful.
And with intention and integrity, your course can deliver either—or both—with confidence.

Chapter 4: Building Your Curriculum – Course by Course, Year by Year

When designing your training programs, it's important to understand that each individual course—even if it's part of a larger program—needs to stand alone as a teachable, certifiable unit.

Single Courses (Certificates)

- Can be taught on their own or as a *module* within a larger diploma.
- Must include:
    - Clear learning outcomes
    - Defined assessment methods
    - A minimum number of instructional hours (varies by modality and association)
    - A certificate of completion
- Can range from a weekend workshop to a full 4- to 12-week course.

- Ideal for continuing education or standalone skills like:
    o Aromatherapy
    o Reflexology
    o Reiki Levels
    o Business Foundations

Tip: These short-format offerings are great for testing demand, earning income quickly, and building toward a full diploma.

Diploma Program Structure (Yearly Levels)

Diplomas are typically broken into logical progressions, often by year or level. For example:

Year 1 / Level 1 (Foundations – 1 to 12 months)

- Focus: Basic techniques, safety, intro theory
- Outcome: Certificate per course + entry-level certification
- Common titles:
    o "Foundations of Massage"
    o "Introduction to Esthetics"
    o "Business & Ethics for Wellness Practitioners"

Year 2 / Level 2 (Intermediate – 12 to 24 months total)

- Builds on foundational knowledge
- Introduces:
    o More complex techniques
    o Anatomy & physiology
    o Case studies and client practicum
- Students often begin with supervised hands-on experience

Year 3 / Level 3 (Advanced – 24 to 36 months total)

- Deep dive into:
    o Advanced assessment
    o Specialized treatment plans
    o Modalities (e.g., Sports Massage, Advanced Aromatherapy)
- Business and marketing modules may be included
- May include externships or internships

Year 4 / Level 4+ (Professional Mastery)

- Reserved for:
    o Advanced specializations
    o Teaching credentials
    o Supervisory or mentorship roles
- Sometimes leads to the title of "Master Practitioner" or "Instructor Certification"

Courses Within Programs

Even if you're offering a full diploma, you'll need to clearly outline and separate:

- Each individual course/module
- Total program hours vs course hours
- Whether students can take individual courses à la carte

In Summary

Whether you're teaching a single weekend workshop or a four-year professional diploma, your structure should be:

1. Modular and stackable
2. Transparent and documented
3. Outcome-based and certifiable

Students—and regulators—should always be able to trace the learning path from first class to graduation.

Shared Core Courses Within Multi-Certificate Programs

When designing a program that includes multiple individual certificate courses, it's important to recognize that not every subject needs to be taught repeatedly. Certain foundational subjects—like *Anatomy & Physiology, Business Fundamentals, Ethics, or Pathology*—often apply across many modalities or specialties. These are called core courses.

What Are Core Courses?

Core courses are central, required classes that serve as a prerequisite or common foundation for several certifications within a broader program. Once a student completes a core course, it typically does not need to be repeated for each individual certificate.

Why Use Core Courses?

- Efficiency: Students save time and tuition by not duplicating learning.
- Consistency: Every student in your school receives a strong foundational education, regardless of their chosen path.
- Accreditation & Insurance Readiness: These topics are often required by associations and insurers to ensure students meet minimum standards of training.
- Transferability: In some cases, these courses may also be recognized by other institutions or associations, increasing the value of your curriculum.

Examples of Common Core Courses:

- **Anatomy & Physiology:** Often required for massage, esthetics, energy work, body therapies, etc.
- **Pathology:** Important for understanding contraindications and safe practice.
- **Business & Ethics:** Essential for launching and managing a professional practice in any wellness field.
- **Sanitation & Hygiene:** Especially for spa, beauty, and hands-on modalities.

How to Implement This in Your School:

- List the core courses separately within your program materials.
- Clearly state which certificates require each core course.
- Track student progress so they only complete each one once.
- Ensure your student contracts and course outlines reflect shared credit where applicable.
- If offering modular enrollment, let students know upfront what they can "carry forward" into future certificates.

Example:

A student takes:

- Reiki Level 1 Certificate
- Reflexology Certificate
- Aromatherapy Certificate

Rather than repeating *Anatomy & Physiology* three times, they take it once, and it fulfills a requirement for all three.

Tip: If you plan to register with associations or accreditation bodies, ensure your shared core structure is clearly documented and justified.

Using Academic Titles: Bachelor's, Master's, Doctorate, and Ph.D.

These academic degree titles are protected by law in many jurisdictions. Not just anyone—or any school—can offer programs that use them. Here's what you need to know:

Protected Terms in Most Countries:

The following titles are often legally protected and can only be used by recognized, government-authorized institutions:

- Diploma (sometimes restricted at certain levels)
- Associate Degree
- Bachelor's Degree
- Master's Degree
- Doctorate (Doctor of ...)
- Ph.D. (Doctor of Philosophy)

To legally use these terms in your courses or credentials, your school typically must be:

A government-accredited institution, Approved by a recognized degree-granting authority, and Listed with a national or provincial ministry of education or a higher learning body.

Who Can Use These Titles?

1. Universities

- Government-chartered institutions
- Can grant all levels of academic degrees (BA, MA, Ph.D.)
- Must meet strict academic, research, and faculty standards

2. Colleges (Degree-Granting)

- In some provinces or countries, certain colleges are granted degree-awarding powers
- These are regulated just like universities

3. Private Career Colleges / Unregulated Schools

- Cannot offer Bachelor's, Master's, or Doctoral degrees
- Can offer certificates and diplomas, as long as those words are permitted in your jurisdiction
- If you want to teach advanced material, you can use terms like:
  - *Advanced Diploma*
  - *Practitioner Level I/II/III*
  - *Instructor Training*
  - *Master-Level Course* (not the same as a Master's degree)

Consequences of Misuse

Using restricted titles without proper authorization can result in:

- Legal action from your province/state or education authority
- Fines or school closure
- Lawsuits from misled students
- Loss of insurance coverage for your graduates

What About Natural Health or Spiritual Degrees?

Some natural medicine or holistic healing schools (especially from the USA or online) offer *Doctor of Natural Medicine* or *Ph.D. in Metaphysics* degrees. These may be considered:

- Unaccredited religious or private degrees, and
- Not legally recognized in most mainstream professional settings

In Canada, for example, calling yourself a "Doctor" without being licensed by a regulated health college (like chiropractors or naturopaths) can be illegal under healthcare legislation—*even if you have a legitimate doctorate from a private school.*

In Summary

Only accredited or government-recognized schools can issue degrees like:

- Bachelor's
- Master's
- Doctorate
- Ph.D.

If your school is private or non-accredited, you should avoid those titles entirely. Instead, focus on issuing certificates, diplomas, or practitioner designations that are:

- Legitimate
- Ethical
- Clear to the public

And if you ever want to expand into degree-level education, be prepared to go through a rigorous government application and audit process to become authorized.

To Become a University

An institution must meet strict criteria and go through a formal approval process governed by national or provincial/state authorities, depending on the country. Here's how it generally works for English-speaking countries:

CA Canada

In Canada, education is regulated at the provincial/territorial level, so each province has its own process.

To become a *university* in Canada, you must:

1. Be authorized by provincial legislation – A private or public university must be created or recognized by a provincial act or ministerial designation.

2. Meet quality assurance standards – Each province has a quality assurance body (e.g., Ontario's Postsecondary Education Quality Assessment Board - PEQAB, or BC's Degree Quality Assessment Board - DQAB).

3. Be authorized to grant degrees – Only institutions approved under legislation can use terms like *Bachelor's, Master's, Doctorate.*

4. Use of the word "university" is protected – You cannot use the word "university" in your business or school name unless officially approved. Doing so is a legal violation.

US United States

In the U.S., recognition of a university is typically managed by state-level education departments plus regional/national accreditation bodies.

Requirements include:

1. State licensure – Permission to operate as an educational institution.
2. Authorization to confer degrees – Usually by a state higher education authority.
3. Accreditation – To be recognized as a legitimate university, most institutions seek accreditation from recognized bodies (e.g., Middle States Commission, WASC).
4. Title usage – Using the term "university" without meeting regulatory and accreditation standards is illegal or misleading in most states.

GB United Kingdom

To be a university in the UK:

1. Must be granted university status by the Privy Council (based on advice from the Department for Education).
2. Must offer a range of degree programs and meet quality assurance benchmarks by the Quality Assurance Agency (QAA).
3. Protected titles: "University," "University College," and "College of Higher Education" are legally protected.

AU Australia

In Australia:

1. Universities are regulated by TEQSA – the Tertiary Education Quality and Standards Agency.
2. A provider must be registered as a "Higher Education Provider" and meet the Higher Education Standards Framework.
3. The use of "university" is restricted and protected under law.
4. The Minister for Education grants final approval, often upon TEQSA's recommendation.

Summary: Who Can Call Themselves a "University"?

- Must be government-approved and authorized to grant degrees.
- The title "university" is legally protected in most countries.
- Institutions using the title without proper authorization can face legal action, fines, and shutdown.

If you're a private educator or school owner, your path may be to:

- Start with certificate and diploma programs.
- Expand into multi-year professional programs.
- Partner with or seek recognition from an existing degree-granting institution or apply for ministerial approval to offer degrees (if possible in your jurisdiction).

To Become a College

Also involves government oversight, though it's generally more accessible than obtaining university status. However, the use of the word "college" is still regulated and protected by law in most jurisdictions. Below is how it works in major English-speaking regions:

CA Canada

In Canada, "college" is a protected title. You cannot use it in your school name unless approved by the provincial government.

Who can be a "college" in Canada?

1. **Public Colleges** – Examples: George Brown College, Okanagan College
   o Created and funded by the provincial government.
   o Governed under provincial legislation (e.g., Ontario Colleges of Applied Arts and Technology Act).
2. **Private Career Colleges (PCCs)** –
   o Must register with the appropriate provincial authority (e.g., PTIB in BC, PEQAB in Ontario).
   o Allowed to use "college" only if approved and follow all compliance requirements.
   o Must offer vocational or career-training programs.
3. **Unregulated Private Schools** –

- ○ Cannot use "college" unless approved.
- ○ May only call themselves "academy," "training centre," or similar titles.

Protected Title Laws:

- In British Columbia: You must register and/or be certified by the Private Training Institutions Branch (PTIB) to use the term "college."
- In Ontario: Must be registered with the Superintendent of Private Career Colleges.

US United States

In the U.S., the term "college" is less tightly restricted than "university," but still regulated depending on the state.

To legally call yourself a "college," you must:

1. Be licensed by your state's Department of Education or equivalent body.
2. Offer academic or vocational programs that meet state criteria.
3. Some states require accreditation to use the term "college."
4. Certain words like "community college" or "junior college" are often restricted to public institutions.

Example: You can't call your online course platform "California College of Energy Healing" without permission.

GB United Kingdom

In the UK, "college" is also a regulated term, although less so than "university."

1. Colleges can be:
   o Further Education (FE) Colleges (vocational training after secondary school)
   o Sixth Form Colleges (focused on A-levels)
   o Independent Colleges (private, may prepare students for university)
2. To use the name legally:
   o Must register with the Companies House and
   o May need to be listed with the UK Register of Learning Providers.
3. Some private training organizations call themselves "colleges," but must ensure it's not misleading.

AU Australia

In Australia:

1. Registered Training Organisations (RTOs) can apply to use the word "college."
   o Must be approved by ASQA (Australian Skills Quality Authority).
2. Use of the term "college" is restricted under the National Vocational Education and Training Regulator Act 2011.
3. Misuse of the term can lead to:
   o Fines

     o Deregistration
     o Public notices of non-compliance

Other English-Speaking Countries (e.g., South Africa, Nigeria, Kenya)

- The use of "college" is usually regulated by the Ministry of Education or Higher Education Authority.
- You must register with a governing body and demonstrate:
  - o Curriculum quality
  - o Qualified instructors
  - o Financial and operational compliance

Summary: Who Can Use "College"?

Region	"College" Use Regulated?	Must Be Registered?	Notes
Canada	Yes ✓	Yes ✓	PTIB or provincial body approval required
United States	Yes (state-dependent) ✓	Often ✓	Can be stricter for accredited status
United Kingdom	Yes ✓	Yes ✓	Must not mislead public
Australia	Yes ✓	Yes ✓	RTO registration with ASQA
Africa	Yes ✓	Yes ✓	Governed by each country's Ministry of Education

Key Takeaways:

- You must get approval to use the word "college" legally.
- It's NOT just a marketing term—it's a legal designation tied to the type of education, compliance, and student protections you offer.
- Using it without permission can lead to:
  - Fines
  - Forced rebranding
  - Loss of credibility and trust

Are Unregistered "Colleges" Legal?

In short: No, unless they meet very specific exceptions. But enforcement varies wildly.

The Legal Reality

In most English-speaking countries, including Canada, the U.S., UK, and Australia:

"College" is a protected term—meaning you cannot legally use it in your business name unless you've:

- Registered with the appropriate government regulatory body
- Been granted permission to use the term based on your educational structure

For example, in British Columbia, you must be registered or certified by the Private Training Institutions Branch (PTIB) to call yourself a college—even if you're unaccredited.

So why are there still schools using "college" that aren't registered?

Here's why:

1. Grandfathered Institutions

- If a school existed before regulations changed (e.g., pre-PCTIA/PTIB rules), it *may* have been grandfathered in.
- However, even those schools often had to meet certain criteria to retain the name.
- Moving locations or changing ownership usually nullifies grandfathering.

2. Lack of Enforcement

- In practice, not every city or province monitors school names unless:
    o A complaint is made
    o A student sues
    o They apply for a license or funding
- Some "colleges" slip through the cracks, especially if they don't issue diplomas or student tax forms, or operate in niche or spiritual markets.

3. Use of Loopholes

- Some schools register as a business under a different name, then use "College" only in marketing or on a website (not on legal documents).
- This is technically misleading and could be shut down if reported.

4. International Schools Operating in Canada

- Schools based outside Canada may use "college" in their brand without realizing it's protected here.
- If they teach students *in Canada*, they're still subject to Canadian rules.

The Risks of Using "College" Without Approval

If you use "college" without permission:

- You can receive a cease and desist letter
- Be forced to rebrand at your own cost
- Get fined or even sued for misrepresentation
- Lose student trust or insurance eligibility

How to Stay Safe

If you're not a government-registered school, use alternative terms:

- Academy
- Institute
- Training Centre
- School (sometimes restricted, depending on context)
- Studio or Workshop (if informal)

Final Word

Just because others are doing it doesn't mean it's legal—or smart.

If you're building a professional, trustworthy school with plans to grow, start with a name you won't have to fight to keep.

Course Credits for Associations: What You Need to Know

Why Register Courses with Associations?

Professional associations exist to maintain industry standards, support their members, and ensure continuing education meets a minimum level of quality. If you want your students or graduates to:

- Earn CEUs (Continuing Education Units) or professional development credits
- Meet association renewal requirements
- Get insurance or business licensing based on their education
- Teach your course and have it recognized

…then your course likely needs to be pre-approved and registered with the relevant association(s).

Who Requires Association-Approved Credits?

- Massage therapists
- Estheticians
- Holistic practitioners (e.g., Reiki, reflexology, aromatherapy)
- Fitness professionals
- Nutritionists
- Mental health coaches/counselors
- Spa therapists

Each profession and association will have its own rules, but most follow a similar approval model.

Steps to Register Your Course with an Association

1. ## Choose the Right Association(s)
   - o Select the one(s) that align with your industry and target students.
   - o Example: Reflexology Association of Canada (RAC), Canadian Reiki Association (CRA), NHPC, Canadian Massage Therapy Alliance, etc.

2. ## Prepare Your Course Materials
   Most associations will ask for:
   - o Course outline and objectives
   - o Total hours (in-class, online, or hybrid)
   - o Instructor bio/resume
   - o Assessment or evaluation method
   - o Delivery method (live, video, hands-on, etc.)
   - o Certificate of completion sample
   - o Proof of your school/business registration

3. ## Submit an Application
   - o Some use online portals, others require email or hard copy applications.
   - o Include a **non-refundable fee** (often between $50–$500 depending on the association and course length).

4. ## Wait for Approval
   - o This can take a few weeks to a few months.
   - o You may receive an approval letter, listing in their CEU course directory, and permission to use their logo.

5. ## Maintain Active Status
   - o Approvals may expire (e.g., 1–3 years).
   - o You may need to re-submit or pay annual listing fees.
   - o Be sure to **report student completions** if required.

What Students Need to Know

Make it clear in your marketing if your course:

- Is recognized by their association
- Offers official CEUs or continuing education credits
- Meets renewal or licensing requirements
- Is instructor-approved, school-approved, or course-approved

Potential Pitfalls

- Claiming CEUs without approval can result in:
  o Student complaints or refund demands
  o Association sanctions against the practitioner
  o Legal issues for deceptive advertising
- Not updating course content after approval (especially when association standards change)
- Association-specific limitations: Some only accept live classes, others accept online training, and a few limit who can teach.

Owning the Course vs. Teaching Another's

- If you created the course, you can register it under your name or your school's.
- If you are licensed to teach someone else's curriculum, ensure they allow you to apply for CEU credit (some associations only accept the course creator).

Additional Best Practices

- Register with multiple associations to expand reach.
- Offer different course levels (e.g., beginner, advanced, trainer) and register each.
- Keep student completion records for at least 5–7 years for audit purposes.
- Offer a clear certificate with:
  - Course name
  - Total hours
  - Instructor name
  - Date of completion
  - Your school's name and contact info

In Summary

Registering your courses with professional associations:

- Builds credibility
- Ensures student eligibility for CEUs and insurance
- Expands your reach and trust factor
- Keeps you aligned with industry standards

But it comes with responsibility—be prepared to maintain compliance, update materials, and track student completions.

Who Can Register Courses with Professional Associations?

You Don't Always Need to Be an Accredited School

In most cases, you do not need to be government-accredited to register a course with an association. What matters more is:

- The quality and clarity of your course
- Your professional credentials or experience in the field
- The association's internal policies

Many associations welcome independent trainers, certified practitioners, and non-accredited schools—as long as the course aligns with their standards.

Who *Can* Apply to Register a Course:

1. **Independent Practitioners or Trainers**
   - If you have enough professional experience, you can often submit your own course for approval.
2. **Unaccredited Schools or Wellness Centers**
   - You can still register courses, especially if you provide student outcomes, a clear scope of practice, and have public liability insurance.
3. **Accredited Colleges or Institutions**
   - These are sometimes fast-tracked or pre-approved, but accreditation is *not* always required.
4. **Course Creators or Modalities Developers**

    o   If you've developed a new technique, you can often apply for your course to be registered as its own modality or continuing ed option.

Some Associations *Do* Have Requirements:

While most associations don't require government accreditation, they might still ask for:

- A registered business license
- Instructor's certifications or diplomas
- Course outline and learning objectives
- A sample certificate of completion
- A minimum number of training hours
- A professional liability insurance policy

Example:

- The Reflexology Association of Canada (RAC) allows unaccredited schools to register courses for continuing education, as long as the course is relevant and the instructor is qualified.
- The Canadian Reiki Association accepts Reiki Masters (not necessarily from accredited schools) to register their Reiki training levels for recognition.
- The NHPC (Natural Health Practitioners of Canada) reviews CEU courses submitted by practitioners, regardless of whether the school is accredited.

Bottom Line:

You do not need to be an accredited school to register courses for association approval.

But you do need to:

- Be qualified
- Offer a clear, legitimate course
- Follow the association's submission process and guidelines

Chapter 5: Student Experience = Your Reputation

Student Expectations & Results: What Are They Really Getting?

When a student enrolls in your course or program—whether online, hybrid, or in-person—they're not just buying information. They're investing in an experience, a transformation, and a tangible result.

What Students Expect:

Most students don't know the ins and outs of accreditation or regulatory law. Instead, they ask themselves:

- *Will I get certified at the end?*
- *Can I start working or offering this service after I graduate?*
- *Will I be confident and capable of doing what I've been taught?*
- *Will I be able to get insurance or a business licence?*
- *Will this help me change my life, income, or career path?*

Their expectations are results-based—not legalese-based.

What Makes *Your* Course or School Unique?

You must clearly communicate the value proposition of your offering. This is what sets your course or school apart from free YouTube tutorials or generic learning platforms.

Consider the following:

1. Real-World Application

- Your course is designed for practical, real-life use— whether in starting a business, getting clients, or offering healing services.
- You teach what actually works in a clinical, spa, or entrepreneurial setting.

2. Hands-On Transformation

- Your students don't just *learn*—they *do*.
- Case studies, feedback, mentorship, and live practice sessions are built in (where applicable).
- You support adult learners with different styles (visual, auditory, kinesthetic, logical).

3. Ethical Framework & Scope of Practice

- You don't just train technique—you teach integrity, communication, consent, and boundaries.
- Your students graduate knowing how to practice safely, legally, and professionally.

4. Legacy Wisdom

- Your content is based on years—sometimes decades—of real client work, industry experience, or traditional knowledge.

- This isn't copy-paste curriculum. It's lived experience passed down with purpose.

5. Business Preparation

- Many holistic or trade-focused students want to *work for themselves.*
- If you include marketing, client attraction, or business setup guidance, you've added an invaluable bonus.

Set Clear, Honest Outcomes

Be specific in your marketing, website, and intake materials. For example:

- "Graduates will receive a certificate of completion and be eligible to apply for liability insurance through [XYZ Association]."
- "This course does not lead to provincial licensing but offers practical tools to build your own healing practice ethically and confidently."

Final Tip:

Students care less about your accreditation status and more about how empowered, confident, and prepared they feel when they graduate.

If you can deliver on that—and prove it through testimonials and student success stories—you'll build lasting trust and a powerful reputation.

Designing Transformation, Not Just Information

Why Good Teaching Changes Lives— Not Just Minds

You've probably taken a course before that was... fine. The instructor was knowledgeable. The materials were organized. The content made sense.

But when it was over, you felt pretty much the same.
A bit smarter, maybe—but not changed.

That's the difference between information and transformation.

If your goal is to truly make a difference—to teach something meaningful that others can carry into their lives or careers—then your course must offer more than facts.

It must offer **a shift**.

What Is a Transformational Course?

A transformational course doesn't just answer questions.
It changes how the student:

- Sees themselves
- Moves through the world
- Approaches their practice or profession
- Uses their new skills to serve others

In other words, it turns *learning* into *becoming*.

A reflexology student doesn't just memorize pressure points—
they gain the confidence to help relieve pain.
A Reiki student doesn't just learn hand positions—they walk away
with the ability to channel healing energy.
A brow design student doesn't just learn technique—they begin to
see themselves as an artist with value and purpose.

That's transformation.

How to Design for Transformation

Here's how to infuse your course with the kind of energy that shifts your students—not just educates them.

1. Know Their "Before and After"

Define:

- Where your student is emotionally, mentally, or skill-wise before they begin
- Where you want them to be by the end

Write it out like this:

Before: unsure, inconsistent, guessing
After: confident, consistent, practicing with intention

This becomes the soul of your course.

2. Layer Knowledge with Experience

Transformation happens through *application.*

For every concept you teach, ask:

- How can they use this in real life?
- What practice will help them internalize it?
- What reflection will help them see their own growth?

Examples:

- Teach the technique → assign a case study
- Share a principle → include a journal prompt
- Demonstrate a skill → ask for a student video demo

3. Celebrate Small Wins

Break big breakthroughs into smaller milestones.

People stay motivated when they feel progress.
Consider including:

- Badges or checkmarks for completed modules
- Certificates for mini-milestones (ex. "Level 1 Complete")
- Encouraging messages when students finish assignments or reach goals

4. Create a Supportive Container

Students need to feel safe to transform.
That means:

- Clear communication
- Realistic expectations
- Encouragement
- A way to reach out for support

This isn't about being available 24/7—it's about being intentional.
Whether you run live sessions or offer automated support, your students should feel **seen, respected, and guided.**

Final Word for This Section:

A good course teaches information.
A great course creates transformation.

You're not just passing on knowledge—you're helping someone *become* the next version of themselves.

Design your program like it matters.
Because it does.

Supporting Adult Learners

Learning Styles, Motivation & Feedback That Makes a Difference

Creating a great course isn't just about what you *teach*—it's about how your students *learn*. And adult learners aren't like high school or college students. They come with real-life experience, responsibilities, fears, habits—and usually, a very personal reason for taking your course.

Teaching adults isn't about control—it's about connection, clarity, and confidence.

Let's explore how to support your students in a way that makes learning stick—and leads to lasting transformation.

Understanding Adult Learning Styles

Not everyone learns the same way. Adults especially tend to have a *preferred learning channel*, based on how they've processed information throughout life.

Here are four common learning styles (which you can integrate into every course):

1. Visual Learners

- Learn best through images, diagrams, videos, and demonstrations
- Benefit from handouts, checklists, and visual models

How to support them: Use charts, slides, illustrations, or recorded demos

2. Auditory Learners

- Learn best by listening and speaking
- Retain information through discussion, storytelling, or audio lectures

How to support them: Add voiceovers, share personal stories, offer group calls or recordings

3. Kinesthetic (Hands-On) Learners

- Learn best by doing—physically engaging with material
- Need to move, touch, or experience the learning

How to support them: Include practice assignments, role play, physical demonstrations, and in-person workshops (if possible)

4. "Knower" or Reflective Learners

- Need time to process, reflect, and understand the *why*
- Prefer structured frameworks and logical explanation

How to support them: Provide journaling prompts, deeper context, and structured modules

Most adults are a mix of these styles.

The best courses touch on all four—so every student feels supported.

The Power of Feedback Loops

Adult learners crave acknowledgment and direction. Without feedback, they often:

- Second-guess themselves
- Delay taking action
- Feel disconnected or unmotivated

Here's how to build meaningful feedback into your course:

Self-Checkpoints:

- Offer quizzes or checklists at the end of each module
- Let them track their own progress (ex. "Can you now name all 7 chakras?")

Instructor Feedback:

- Use simple rubrics to assess submissions
- Send short written comments or audio replies (it feels personal!)
- Offer encouragement as much as critique

Peer or Group Feedback:

- Create space for group review or sharing (especially in longer courses)
- Encourage students to support one another—this builds community and retention

Motivation: Why Adults Actually Stick With It

Adult learners are purpose-driven. They're taking your course because:

- They want a better life
- They want to help others
- They want to start a business or practice
- They're seeking personal healing or growth

Your job as an instructor is to keep connecting the daily learning back to the bigger purpose.

Try reinforcing:

- Why each module matters
- How today's lesson will help them achieve their goal
- What they'll miss out on if they don't stay engaged

This is what keeps them coming back—even when life gets in the way.

Final Thought: Supporting adult learners isn't about doing more.
It's about teaching with empathy, structure, and respect.

Meet them where they are.
Support how they learn.
Remind them why they started.

And they'll not only complete your course—they'll remember you for life.

Checklist for Enrolling International Students

Welcoming international students to your school can be incredibly rewarding—diversifying your student body, expanding your reach, and boosting revenue. But it also comes with legal responsibilities, regulatory oversight, and logistical considerations.

Below is a checklist to help you ensure you're legally and ethically prepared to support international students—especially in regulated training environments.

1. Legal Requirements to Enroll International Students (In-Class)

✔ Ensure your school is a Designated Learning Institution (DLI) approved if operating in Canada and offering study permits
→ *Only DLIs can enroll students on a Canadian study visa. This is typically only granted to accredited institutions that meet strict compliance requirements.*

✔ Confirm your programs meet eligibility criteria (full-time, minimum length, diploma/certificate granting)

✔ Register your institution with IRCC (Immigration, Refugees and Citizenship Canada) if offering visa-eligible programs

2. Immigration Implications

✓ Clearly state whether your program qualifies for a Study Permit
→ *Many short-term or online-only programs do not.*
→ Misleading claims can result in severe penalties and school blacklisting.

✓ Offer acceptance letters with standardized language required for visa applications (if applicable)

✓ Be aware of visa restrictions, such as:

- Work permit eligibility (co-op or post-graduation)
- Required in-person attendance
- Financial proof requirements

✓ Avoid suggesting permanent residency outcomes unless certified to do so through legal immigration counsel

3. English Proficiency & Language Requirements

✓ Establish minimum standards for English (or French) proficiency
→ Use standardized tests like IELTS, TOEFL, Duolingo, or your own in-house placement test

✓ Include language expectations clearly in your student handbook and on your website

✓ Consider offering ESL bridging programs or partnerships for students who need additional support

4. Housing and Student Support

✓ Have a referral or system in place for safe, legal housing
→ *You are not required to provide housing, but you should guide students to reputable host families, homestay agencies, or student housing options*

✓ Provide a welcome package with:

- Local transport options (bus route maps, student discounts)
- Emergency contacts and health services
- Cultural norms and legal rights in Canada

✓ Consider mental health and cultural integration support, such as partnerships with community centers or counselors

5. Fair Tuition & Payment Expectations

✓ Ensure your tuition is fair and transparent
→ Charging international students *significantly more* for identical content (in non-degree programs) may violate consumer protection laws

✓ Provide written refund policies in advance
→ Required under consumer laws and often by immigration offices

✓ Offer multiple payment options (international credit cards, wire transfers, Flywire, etc.)

✓ Remember: International students often have stricter proof of payment and admission documentation needs— prepare accordingly

BONUS TIP:

Keep immigration and enrollment records secure
→ Use Canadian servers or PIPEDA-compliant cloud storage
→ Maintain student records for a minimum of 5–7 years in case of audit

Final Thought:

Enrolling international students isn't just about filling seats—it's about fostering trust, meeting obligations, and making sure students from around the world feel supported and respected.

Why Should They Choose *Your* School? Questionnaire

In a world filled with workshops, certifications, and online programs, students have options—and they're more discerning than ever.

So why should someone choose your school over another?

It's not just about what you teach. It's about the *experience* you offer, the *credibility* you carry, and the *transformation* you deliver.

Use the questions below to define what makes your school stand out—and what areas you might still need to strengthen.

Self-Reflection Questionnaire: What Makes Your School the Right Choice?

1. What transformation does your course promise?

What will students be able to do, know, or feel differently after attending?

2. What proof do you have that your method works?

Testimonials? Case studies? Results from previous students?

3. Do you offer real-world application—not just theory?

Hands-on practice, case studies, client experience?

4. Is your curriculum structured and professional?

Do you use learning outcomes, a syllabus, clear assessment tools, and supporting materials?

5. Is your certificate meaningful?

Can students use it for insurance, business licenses, or credibility in your industry?

6. What makes your teaching style or philosophy unique?

Do you incorporate holistic practices, cultural wisdom, or a specific framework?

7. Are you legally compliant?

Do you meet city, provincial/state, and association standards? (Even if the course is unregulated?)

8. What kind of support do you offer after training?

Mentorship? Alumni networks? Continuing education?

9. Do you have a professional online presence?

A clean website, current branding, clear contact information?

10. Would *you* choose your school over another—if you were the student?
If not, why not?

Tip: Turn Your Answers Into Your Marketing Message

Once you've filled out this questionnaire, look at your strongest answers. These become your:

- Website copy
- Social media messaging
- Course description hooks
- Orientation day talking points

Be clear. Be honest. And always ask yourself:

Would I feel confident enrolling my own child, spouse, or best friend in this school?

If the answer is yes—you're ready.

Part 2: The Legal & Business Side of Starting a School

Chapter 6: Name Search

The Importance of Choosing the Right Name for Your School or Program

Your school's name is more than just a label—it's the *first impression*, the *emotional connection*, and often the *determining factor* in whether a potential student clicks, calls, or enrolls.

Why Your Name Matters:

1. ## Legitimacy & Trust
   - A professional, well-chosen name immediately signals credibility.
   - Names like *"Institute," "Academy," "College," or "Centre"* can imply a structured, serious approach—just make sure they align with your legal status (some provinces restrict the use of "college" or "university" to accredited institutions).
2. ## Searchability & SEO
   - A clear, specific name helps you get found online.
   - If you're teaching Reiki, a name like "Harmonic Healing Institute" is better than something vague like "SoulSpace."
   - Avoid overly trendy or obscure names that don't explain what you do.

3. ## Brand Positioning

   o   Your name should match your tone: Are you
       scientific, spiritual, artistic, clinical, or business-
       oriented?

   o   Example: *"The Integrative Wellness School"* vs. *"The
       Sacred Lotus Temple"*—very different vibes, different
       audiences.

4. ## Avoiding Legal Trouble

   o   Always search local and national business registries
       to avoid duplicating or infringing on another
       company's name.

   o   If possible, secure the matching domain name
       (.com, .ca, etc.) and social media handles.

   o   Check if your name is *too close* to a regulated or
       trademarked institution—especially when using
       terms like "academy," "college," or "certified."

5. ## Growth & Legacy

   o   Think long-term. Will your name still make sense
       if you expand into new services or provinces?

   o   Can someone else take over your brand, license it,
       or franchise it in the future?

Quick Checklist for Naming Your School or Program

- Is it clear and memorable?
- Does it reflect what you teach?
- Is it legally usable in your province/country?
- Can you get the domain and social handles?
- Does it resonate emotionally with your ideal student?

Final Thought:

Choosing the right name is a foundational step in building a
school that feels solid, aligned, and inspiring. Don't rush it—let
your name speak for the values and vision you want your
education to represent.

Double-Check: Is Your Name or Acronym Already Taken?

Choosing the *perfect* name is only the beginning. The next step is making sure no one else is already using it—or something *confusingly similar.*

Why It's Critical:

- **Legal Protection:** Using a name already registered or trademarked could lead to lawsuits, cease-and-desist orders, or forced rebranding.
- **Brand Confusion:** If your acronym or school name is already in use, students may enroll in the wrong place or mistake you for another organization.
- **SEO Competition:** You want your school to be the *first result* when someone Googles your name—not buried under another business or unrelated site.

How to Check for Availability

1. ## Google Search (and Variations)
   - Type your name and acronym in quotes: "Inner Light Institute" or "ILI"
   - Try combinations like:
     - "ILI school"
     - "ILI training Canada"
     - "ILI wellness certification"
     - "Inner Light Institute education"
   - Do this for *both your full name and acronym.*
2. ## Business Name Registries
   - Check your **provincial or state corporate registry** for business names already registered.
   - In Canada:_Nuans Name Search https://www.nuans.com/

- o In the U.S.: Check your state's Secretary of State website.
- o In the UK: Companies House
- o In Australia: ASIC

3. ## Domain Search
    - o Use a site like GoDaddy https://www.godaddy.com/en-ca or Namecheap https://www.namecheap.com/ to search for your ideal web domain.
    - o If the domain is taken, check what kind of business owns it.

4. ## Social Media Handle Search
    - o Use a handle checker like Namecheckr or KnowEm to find out if your name is available on major platforms (Instagram, Facebook, TikTok, etc.).

5. ## Trademark Database
    - o In Canada: CIPO
    - o In the U.S.: USPTO TESS
    - o In the UK: IPO Trademark Search

Don't Assume—Verify

Even if a name "feels unique," acronyms especially can be problematic. You don't want to name your school Global Holistic Education Academy and later find out GHEA is already a certification body in another field—or worse, something controversial or unrelated.

Pro Tip:

If you find a similar name, ask:

- Is it in a *different industry or country*?
- Will it *confuse* your students or clients?

- Are they using it *actively* or is it a dead site?

If you're unsure, consult a business lawyer or branding expert before moving forward.

Common Terms for Educational Institutions

Here's a breakdown of commonly used terms related to educational institutions, including their meanings, legal implications, and who is allowed to use them depending on region (especially relevant for Canada, the U.S., UK, and similar English-speaking countries):

School

- Definition: A general term for any place where instruction is given.
- Who Can Use It: Anyone, unless specified otherwise by provincial/state law.
- Legal Notes: In Canada and the U.S., the term "school" is often unregulated unless used in specific contexts (e.g., public schools, private K–12 schools).
- Examples: Yoga School, Business School, Beauty School.

Safe to use for private training, online education, and wellness/method-based programs.

Academy

- Definition: Traditionally refers to a place of specialized higher learning.
- Who Can Use It: Often unregulated in Canada and the U.S.
- Legal Notes: May be restricted in some jurisdictions if it causes confusion with government-regulated institutions.

- Examples: Makeup Academy, Art Academy, Wellness Academy.

Widely used in beauty, holistic, and skill-based training industries.

Institute / Institute of Technology

- Definition: Typically indicates focused, career-oriented, or technical education.
- Who Can Use It: Use may be restricted in some jurisdictions.
- Legal Notes:
  - In Canada, terms like "institute" can only be used with approval from the province's Ministry of Education or regulatory body.
  - In the U.S., the rules vary state by state.
- Examples: Institute of Aromatherapy, Healing Institute.

Check provincial/state regulations before using.
May imply formal vocational training.

College

- Definition: Traditionally a post-secondary institution offering diplomas, certificates, or degrees.
- Who Can Use It: Restricted in Canada, the U.S., UK, and Australia.
- Legal Notes:

- o In Canada, using "College" generally requires registration with or approval from the provincial regulator (e.g., PTIB in BC).
- o Unauthorized use may lead to fines or legal action.
- Examples: Not allowed to say "College of Healing" unless approved.

Avoid using unless you are formally accredited or registered.

University

- Definition: An institution offering undergraduate and graduate degrees.
- Who Can Use It: Heavily regulated—requires government charter and degree-granting authority.
- Legal Notes:
    - o In Canada, using "university" without a charter is illegal.
    - o In the U.S., only accredited institutions may use "university."
- Examples: "University of Natural Medicine" would not be legal without authorization.

✖ Do not use unless you are a degree-granting institution authorized by government.

Training Centre / Training Facility

- **Definition**: A neutral term for a place where specific skills or training are offered.
- **Who Can Use It**: Anyone.
- **Legal Notes**: No regulatory restrictions in most places.
- **Examples**: Spa Training Centre, Reflexology Training Facility.

Safe for small private courses or workshops.

Learning Centre

- **Definition**: A space or program for learning; often tutoring or enrichment.
- **Who Can Use It**: Anyone.
- **Legal Notes**: Similar to "school" and typically unregulated.
- **Examples**: Holistic Learning Centre.

Safe and professional sounding, especially for community or niche education.

Seminary / Conservatory / Polytechnic

- **Special Use Terms**: These words typically refer to very specific types of education:
  - **Seminary**: Usually refers to religious or theological training for clergy.
  - **Conservatory**: Reserved for advanced music, dance, or performing arts institutions.

- o Polytechnic: Implies government-recognized vocational and technical training across multiple disciplines.
- Who Can Use Them:
  - o Must be used accurately and, in many jurisdictions, only with approval.
  - o Using these terms without alignment to their traditional meanings can be seen as misleading and may be restricted.
- Legal Notes:
  - o In Canada, UK, Australia, and the U.S., these terms are often reserved for formally recognized institutions or require a certain level of curriculum depth and faculty qualifications.
  - o Use without appropriate credentials can lead to consumer complaints or regulatory scrutiny.

Avoid unless your school legitimately operates within these specialized educational fields and meets the criteria.

Safe Terms Summary

If you're starting a school, academy, or training program and you're not yet accredited, your **safest choices** are:

- School
- Academy
- Training Centre
- Learning Centre
- Institute *(with caution—check regulations)*
- Workshop / Program / Certification Program

These offer the **flexibility** to grow while still presenting your offerings professionally and ethically.

Registering Your School Name: Provincial/State vs. National Considerations

Why Registering Your Name Matters

Registering your business or school name isn't just about professionalism—it's a legal move that protects your brand and gives you the right to operate under that name in a specific jurisdiction. But here's what most new school owners don't realize:

Registering your school in one province or state doesn't give you rights nationwide.

Provincial or State Name Registration

When you register your school or training company name provincially or in your state:

- You're allowed to operate under that name *within that specific province or state.*
- You are not automatically allowed to use the name in other provinces, states, or countries.
- This level of registration provides some basic protection, especially if someone else tries to register a *very similar* name locally.

Examples in Canada:

- BC: BC Registry Services
  https://www.corporateonline.gov.bc.ca/
- Alberta: Alberta Corporate Registry
- Ontario: Ontario Business Registry

Examples in the U.S.:

- Each state's Secretary of State website is the place to start (e.g., California Secretary of State).

Federal/National Name Registration

To protect your school name across the entire country:

- In Canada, file a federal business name registration with Corporations Canada.
  Register here →
- In the U.S., register a federal trademark with the USPTO.
  Start here →
- In the UK, use Companies House and register your trademark through the UKIPO.
- In Australia, register your name with the ASIC and trademark with IP Australia.

What Can Go Wrong If You Don't Register Nationally?

1. Name Conflicts
   Someone else can legally register and use your name in another province or state—even if you've been using it for years.
2. Blocked Expansion
   If you try to open a school, teach students, or offer online courses in another province or country, you may be:
   - Denied business licensing
   - Fined
   - Forced to rename or rebrand

3. Legal Action

If someone else has trademarked the name, they can issue a cease-and-desist—even if *you used it first* but didn't register it nationally.

Legal Name Registration vs Trademark: What's the Difference?

1. Registering Your Business Name

This gives you **permission to use the name** in a specific province/state/country for business purposes.

- **Purpose**: Legally operate under that name.
- **Scope**: Local or national, depending on how and where you register.
- **Protection**: Others in the same province usually can't register the exact same name, but similar names may still be used.

2. Trademarking Your Business Name

This gives you the **exclusive right to use** the name/logo/slogan nationwide (or internationally) in specific industries.

- **Purpose**: Prevent others from using your brand in a confusing or competitive way.
- **Scope**: National or international.
- **Protection**: Enforced by law—if someone uses your name, you can take legal action.

Step-by-Step: Registering a Business Name

CA In Canada (provincial registration):

1. ## Search for name availability:
   - o Use your province's name registry search (e.g., BC: BC Registry Services)
   - o Also, do a Google search and check NUANS for similar names
2. ## Register with your province:
   - o For example:
     - BC: BC Registries (OneStop)
     - Alberta: Corporate Registry (Service Alberta)
     - Ontario: ServiceOntario
3. ## Choose your business structure:
   - o Sole proprietorship, partnership, or incorporation
4. ## Pay registration fee:
   - o Varies by province, usually $40–$100
5. ## Optional: Register federally with Corporations Canada for national operation

Step-by-Step: Trademarking a Name (Canada)

1. ## Check for existing trademarks:
   - o Visit the Canadian Trademarks Database
2. ## Prepare your application:
   - o Include the name, logo (if applicable), and classes of goods/services
3. ## File with the Canadian Intellectual Property Office (CIPO):
   - o Online at https://www.ic.gc.ca
   - o Cost: ~$350 CAD for one class, $100 for each additional class

4. Wait for approval:
- o Takes 12–24 months
- o CIPO examines, publishes, and allows time for opposition before approval

For the U.S. (Trademark):

- Search: USPTO TESS Search
- Register: USPTO Online Filing
- Cost: ~$250–$350 USD per class
- Duration: Protects your mark for 10 years (renewable)

For International Protection:

- Register through WIPO's Madrid System for international trademarks: https://www.wipo.int/madrid/en/

What Happens If You Don't Register or Trademark?

- You may lose your brand name if someone trademarks it first.
- Others can use a similar name and confuse your clients or damage your reputation.
- You may be forced to rebrand—changing your name, domain, logo, and course materials.

What "Per Class" Means

When you apply for a trademark, you must identify the specific types of products or services you want the trademark to protect. Each of these types belongs to a class (there are 45 in total):

- Classes 1–34: Goods (physical products)
- Classes 35–45: Services (education, business, legal services, etc.)

You pay per class, so the more types of services/products you want covered, the higher the cost.

Example for a School

If you are creating a school and educational materials, you may need to file under:

- Class 41 – Education services (e.g., training, courses, workshops)
- Class 9 – Digital products (e.g., PDFs, downloadable eBooks, online videos)
- Class 16 – Printed materials (e.g., workbooks, manuals, journals)
- Class 35 – Business consulting or course licensing (if applicable)

If you file for Class 41 only, you are only protected for services like teaching and workshops. If someone uses your name to sell a book or digital product (Class 9 or 16), they might not be infringing your trademark—unless you also registered those classes.

How It Affects Cost

Each country sets its own price per class:

- Canada (CIPO):
  - ~$350 CAD for the first class
  - ~$100 CAD for each additional class
- U.S. (USPTO):
  - $250–$350 USD per class, depending on filing method

Tip

If you're starting small, file for your core class first (usually Class 41 for schools), and expand as needed. You can always file new applications later.

Additional Points to Mention About Naming Your School

1. Your Name Is Your Brand

- It's more than just a title—it's what people remember, talk about, and Google.
- Choose something easy to pronounce, spell, and remember.
- Avoid overly trendy names that may not age well or limit your future expansion.

2. Don't Use Protected or Misleading Terms

- Terms like "University," "College," "Accredited," and "Certified" may be regulated depending on your region.
- Using them without permission or formal recognition can lead to legal action or forced rebranding.
- In most provinces/states, you cannot use "University" or "College" unless granted permission by the provincial/state Ministry of Education.

3. Check for Trademarks

- Even if the business name is available in your province, it may be trademarked elsewhere.
- This is especially important if you plan to sell online or operate in multiple regions or countries.

4. Avoid Names Too Similar to Existing Schools

- Even if a name isn't registered, if it's too close to an existing, well-known school (e.g., "Healing Light Academy" vs. "Light of Healing Academy"), it may confuse students or raise legal concerns.
- Be distinct.

5. Think About SEO and Domain Availability

- Can people find you easily online?
- Check if your domain name and social handles are available.
- Choose a name that is searchable and doesn't bring up unrelated results (e.g., avoid "Evolve" alone—too broad).

6. Think About Future Growth

- Don't box yourself in (e.g., "Kelowna Lash School" might limit you if you later want to teach facials, PMU, or online).
- Consider using something broad enough to grow, like:
    - "Global Holistic Institute"
    - "The Inner Alchemy Academy"
    - "Essential Training Collective"

7. Secure Matching Elements Right Away

Once you've settled on a name, immediately secure:

- Domain name(s) (preferably .com or .ca/.org)
- Social media handles (Instagram, Facebook, TikTok, LinkedIn)
- Logo and brand kit
- Business license under that name
- Trademark or copyright (if desired)

8. Consider International Implications

- If you plan to offer your courses internationally (especially online), make sure the name doesn't mean something inappropriate or confusing in another language or culture.

Chapter 7: What Makes It a "School" Legally?

Do You Need a Physical Location?

Not every school needs a brick-and-mortar space. Many thriving programs operate fully online or in hybrid formats, using rented classrooms, shared spaces, or even temporary venues for hands-on training. But if you're planning to open a **physical location**—whether it's a full campus, a single classroom, or a wellness clinic-style setup—there are some important things you need to know first.

From zoning laws to safety codes, lease agreements to accessibility requirements, the right space can support your vision—or become a costly roadblock. This section walks you through the **key considerations for choosing, preparing, and legally operating** a physical school location. Whether you're just exploring the idea or ready to sign a lease, this information will help you make smart, sustainable decisions that align with your mission and protect your investment.

When choosing a location for your school, it's not just about finding an affordable space—it's about meeting legal, logistical, and practical needs that support your students and your success. Here's what you must consider:

1. Zoning and Legal Use

- Check with your city hall or municipal office to confirm the space is zoned for *educational or institutional* use.
- If the zoning is for retail or office only, you may need to apply for a rezoning or special use permit, which can take months or be denied.
- Do not sign a lease until you receive written confirmation that your intended use (i.e., running a private training institution or vocational school) is legally permitted.
- Some cities require seismic upgrades, sprinklers, or accessibility improvements for schools—especially if you're planning classroom-based instruction.

2. Size and Layout

- Is there enough space for your intended class sizes, equipment, and student comfort?
- Think about:
    - Dedicated classrooms vs. multi-use rooms
    - Treatment areas for hands-on modalities (e.g., massage, esthetics)
    - A reception/waiting area
    - Storage for supplies and confidential student files
    - Staff office space (especially if you will grow your team)

3. Accessibility

- **Public Transit:** Being near a bus or train line makes your school more accessible to a wider audience—especially younger students or those without vehicles.
- **Parking:** Ensure there is ample, safe, and legal parking available nearby for students, staff, and clients (if you offer public services).
- **Disability Access:** Consider wheelchair ramps, elevators, and accessible washrooms if required.

4. Visibility and Safety

- A well-lit, visible location in a safe neighborhood increases student confidence and walk-in inquiries.
- Locations in professional complexes or wellness centers may boost your credibility compared to stand-alone or industrial zones.
- Consider signage rules—some buildings or cities restrict how large or visible your school sign can be.

5. Lease Terms and Permissions

- Avoid signing a lease that:
  - Ties you down for more years than you're ready to commit
  - Prohibits subletting (if you plan to grow or rent space to instructors)
  - Lacks a business license clause (you want the ability to cancel if the city denies your business license)
- Verify if your insurance provider approves the location for coverage.

6. Affordability and Utilities

- Can you afford the rent and utilities *year-round,* even during slower enrollment seasons?
- Ask about:
    - Heating/cooling costs
    - Internet availability (especially for hybrid or online programs)
    - Shared utility bills in commercial complexes

7. Student Experience

- Are there nearby amenities? (Cafes, grocery, parks, etc.)
- Is the location easy to find with GPS?
- Will students feel safe and welcomed entering and exiting?

Bonus Tip: Paperwork First

Before committing to a lease:

- Get a letter of intent approved by your city zoning officer.
- Apply for your business license early.
- Ensure your insurance policy covers this location.

City Business Licensing

Before your curriculum is even printed, before you enroll your first student, there's one thing every aspiring school owner must face: city business licensing.

It may seem like a formality—but in many cases, it's the very moment that defines your business as a "school" in the eyes of the law.

What Is a City Business License?

A city business license is an official permit that allows you to operate legally within your local municipality. Whether you're renting a commercial space, working from a home-based studio, or offering online education, you'll likely need one.

But here's the twist: how you describe your business can shape everything—from inspections to allowable services.

"Teaching" vs "Practicing"

When applying for your license, you may be asked:

- Are you providing a service (e.g., massage, facials)?
- Or are you teaching a skill?

This distinction matters. In many cities:

- A teaching facility (aka school or training centre) may fall under different zoning bylaws or safety regulations than a personal service business.

- Being classified as a "school" might trigger inspections from the fire department, building code, or even parking and accessibility standards.

Real Example

You walk in hoping to open a healing center—but when you explain that you'll teach weekend Reiki classes?
Suddenly, you're a "school."
That one word changes your classification—and potentially opens the door for you to offer group training, issue certificates, and have classroom setups... as long as you pass the appropriate inspections.

Do You Need a City Business License if You Teach from Home (Including Online)?

In most cities and municipalities, yes, you still need a business license to legally operate a business from your home — even if it's entirely online and no clients ever come to your door.

Here's why:

Home-Based Business = Still a Business

Whether you're:

- Running an online course platform
- Teaching private Zoom classes
- Hosting virtual workshops
- Creating and selling digital course content

… your activities are considered commercial use of your residence, and local governments typically require home-based business licenses to regulate that.

What They May Look At:

- Zoning compliance: Some cities restrict certain business activities in residential zones (even online).
- Parking/traffic impact: Even if students don't visit, package delivery, signage, or occasional foot traffic might trigger review.
- Type of business: Teaching, coaching, and digital services are usually permitted—but it's always best to check your local bylaws.

TIP:

Call or visit your city or municipal website and search for:

- *"Home-based business license"*
- *"Online business license"*
- *"Zoning for home business"*

You'll typically find a short checklist and an application process. Many cities even allow online filing for small business licenses.

Penalties for Non-Compliance:

Operating without a license (even quietly from home) can result in:

- Fines
- Forced closure
- Denial of future permits or grants
- Problems getting business insurance or tax deductions

Key Steps to Take

1. Check zoning laws
   o Is your space zoned for educational activity?
   o If not, can you apply for a variance?
2. Be strategic in your application
   o Use clear, honest language: *"offering private vocational workshops,"* or *"teaching holistic wellness skills"*
   o Avoid vague phrases like "healing space" unless your goal is a clinic.
3. Be ready for inspection
   o Schools may require:
     ▪ Fire extinguishers and emergency lighting
     ▪ Clear exits and posted floorplans
     ▪ Washrooms for students
     ▪ Accessibility compliance
4. Ask about occupancy limits
   o The fire department may place a cap on how many students you can teach at one time.

Renewals & Changes

- Business licenses are usually annual.
- If you move locations or expand your offerings (e.g., add online training or open a second classroom), you may need to update your license or reapply.

In Summary:

A city business license:

- Yes—you usually need a business license, even for home-based or online-only schools. It's a small investment in legitimacy, and it can protect you legally, financially, and professionally as your school grows.
- Makes your school legal in your municipality
- Helps you clarify your operations and responsibilities
- Protects you from future legal or insurance problems
- Is often the first step to turning your knowledge into a real educational business

Zoning and Inspections

(Fire Department, Signage, ADA/Accessibility Compliance)

Once you've secured (or are applying for) your business license, the next legal checkpoints often come in the form of zoning regulations and inspections—especially if your business is being classified as a *school.*

These requirements may vary by city, but the core issues are consistent across most municipalities.

Zoning Laws: Can You Teach There?

Zoning determines what kind of activities are allowed in specific geographic areas.

When opening a school—whether from a storefront, a commercial office, or even your home—you need to confirm:

- ## Is the location zoned for educational use?
  - o "Instructional spaces," "vocational training," or "schools" may fall under a different zoning than personal services or retail.
- ## Home-based teaching?
  - o Many cities restrict foot traffic, noise, or the number of students allowed at one time. You may need a *home occupation permit* and/or a conditional use permit.

If your proposed school isn't aligned with the current zoning, you may need:

- A rezoning application
- A variance request
- Or a temporary use permit

Fire Department Inspections

Schools fall under public assembly guidelines in some municipalities—even small ones. This may trigger an inspection by the fire department, often before your license is approved.

Expect them to check for:

- Fire extinguishers in visible, accessible places
- Clear emergency exits (no locked back doors or clutter)
- Smoke detectors and, in some cases, a fire alarm system
- Clearly posted occupant limits (especially in classroom-style setups)
- A documented fire evacuation plan

Even if your class is four people in a quiet wellness space, if you're open to the public or training others, you may be considered a *public access business*.

Signage Compliance

Want a sign on your building or window that says "Academy," "Training Centre," or "Institute"? Check before you order it.

Many municipalities require:

- ## A sign permit
  - Approval of sign dimensions, lighting, and location
  - Compliance with bylaws around visibility, illumination, or placement (e.g., not obstructing driver views)

Failing to get a sign permit can result in fines—even if your school is otherwise approved.

Accessibility / ADA Compliance (or Regional Equivalent)

Depending on your country or city, you may be required to:

- Ensure entrances are accessible by wheelchair
- Have accessible washrooms
- Include ramps or elevators if located on non-ground floors
- Post clear signage for accessible features

In the U.S., this falls under ADA (Americans with Disabilities Act)

In Canada, there are provincial and municipal accessibility acts

In the UK and Australia, Equality Acts or Access to Premises Standards apply

Even if you're not legally required to make full accessibility upgrades, it's worth doing:

- Ethically, to serve all students
- Practically, as insurance companies may ask about it
- Strategically, to help with future accreditation or funding

Summary Checklist

Before you open your doors:

- Confirm your zoning allows educational use
- Schedule any required inspections (fire, building)
- Plan for accessibility—even if optional
- Get permits for outdoor or window signage
- Post maximum occupancy and fire exit signs

When a "Workshop" Becomes a "School"

You may start out offering a simple weekend class, a Reiki workshop, a DIY facial training, or a breathwork retreat. It's casual. It's heart-led. It feels small.

But legally speaking, at some point that workshop becomes a school—and that's where things shift.

Understanding where that line is drawn can protect you from unexpected legal, zoning, tax, or insurance issues.

What's the Difference?

Let's compare:

Workshop	School
One-time or occasional offering	Ongoing classes or multiple programs
No formal enrollment process	Student intake, registration, policies
No structured evaluation	Assessments, certificates, or exams
Typically held in rented spaces	Operates from a consistent facility
Informal teaching, peer-style	Structured curriculum, learning outcomes

Workshop	School
Not advertising itself as a "school"	Marketed as a training institute, academy, or college

Key Indicators You've Become a "School"

Ask yourself:

- Are you issuing certificates or diplomas?
- Do you have learning outcomes, modules, or tests?
- Are students required to register, pay tuition, or sign contracts?
- Do you market yourself as an institute, college, or academy?
- Do your students need this training for licensing, insurance, or employment?
- Do you run multiple classes or levels (e.g., Level 1, 2, Master)?

If you answered *yes* to even a few of these, you're no longer just offering a "workshop." You're operating a vocational training program or private school—and that means more oversight.

Why It Matters

If you operate like a school but:

- Your business license says you're a service provider (e.g., massage or retail), or
- You don't meet fire/building safety or zoning for education, or
- You're charging tuition and issuing certificates without proper insurance...

You could be:

- Denied future licensing
- Fined or shut down by the city
- Sued by a student with no protection
- Denied insurance claims due to misclassification

Best Practice

If your offering is growing and gaining structure:

Treat it like a school—even if you still call it a workshop.

That way, you build on a strong foundation, stay compliant, and protect your reputation and your students.

Chapter 8: Certificates, Diplomas & Accreditation

The Truth Behind Those Words

(What students think they mean vs. what they actually mean)

Let's be honest—most students don't read the fine print. They see words like *"Certified," "Diploma,"* or *"Accredited School"* and assume one thing:

"This must be official. Recognized. Government-approved. I'll be able to get a job or open a business with this."

But here's the reality…

Those words carry very different meanings, depending on how they're used—and who's using them.

What Students Think They're Getting

When students see terms like:

- Certificate – They think: *"I'm qualified to do this professionally now."*
- Diploma – They think: *"This must be a government-level or industry-approved education."*
- Accredited – They think: *"This school has been vetted and recognized by official education bodies."*

And while that *can* be true, it often isn't—especially in unregulated industries.

What Those Words Actually Mean

Term	Reality Check
Certificate	A record of completion. It means the student took your course. It's not a license.
Diploma	A longer or more advanced program. The term is not legally protected in most regions.
Accredited	This only has weight *if backed by a recognized accrediting body.* Otherwise, it's marketing.

Why This Confusion Matters

Students make career decisions based on assumptions. If your course says "certified" but:

- You're not recognized by a professional association

- Your course doesn't meet industry licensing standards
- You haven't been approved by a government education ministry

Then a student could end up:

- Unable to get insurance
- Denied a business license
- Or worse—misrepresenting their credentials and facing legal consequences

As a course creator, you're responsible for setting the record straight. Transparency builds trust—and protects both you and your students.

Your Responsibility as a School Owner

1. Define your terms clearly in all marketing materials and on certificates.
   o Example: "This certificate represents completion of ___ hours of training in ___."
2. Be honest about what your certificate does *not* provide:
   o It is not a government-issued license.
   o It is not affiliated with regulated industry boards—unless it is.
3. Explain accreditation (or lack of it) and help students understand how to use your training legally and ethically.

Next, we can expand on:

- How to issue meaningful certificates and what to include on them

- The difference between *accreditation*, *recognition*, and *affiliation*
- What to do if your students need insurance or licensing

Provincial/National Association Rules

(Why you can't just make up a title—and how to know if you're crossing a line)

Once your course is built, your curriculum is tight, and students are excited... there's one more critical question:

Can they actually *use* what you've taught them in the real world?

The answer depends on whether their new skills or title fall under the authority of a provincial, national, or industry association.

What Are Associations and Why Do They Matter?

Associations exist to:

- Maintain professional standards
- Protect the public from unqualified practitioners
- Govern the use of titles, scopes of practice, and certification

They may be:

- Government-regulated (e.g., College of Massage Therapists of BC)

- Industry-led (e.g., Canadian Association of Natural Nutrition Practitioners)
- Voluntary, but influential (e.g., Reiki associations or holistic boards)

Some associations are **mandatory to join** if you want to legally use a title. Others offer **optional membership**, but insurance companies, employers, or clients may expect affiliation.

Protected Titles

In Canada (and many other countries), certain titles are **protected by law**, meaning you can't teach a course and issue a certificate that implies someone is one of these unless they've gone through the official, accredited path.

Examples:

- **Massage Therapist (RMT)** – Must be trained through a government-recognized program and registered with a provincial college (e.g., in BC or Ontario)
- **Esthetician** – Often regulated through provincial training/apprenticeship systems
- **Doctor, Nurse, Psychologist, Social Worker,** etc. – All protected titles with strict educational and licensing paths

What You Can Teach and Certify

You can absolutely:

- Teach your unique method or modality
- Issue a certificate of **completion** (not of license or designation)

- Help students start their own **unregulated practice** (e.g., Reiki, life coaching, energy work, wellness workshops)

But you **cannot:**

- Use a protected title without permission or licensing
- Guarantee your students will be eligible for **insurance or business licenses** without verifying association rules
- Market your school in a way that implies government or regulatory recognition if you don't have it

How to Navigate the Association Landscape

1. **Identify whether your course connects to a regulated industry**
   - Check your province/state's governing body for that profession
   - Look up professional associations to understand their scope and rules

2. **Be transparent in your course descriptions**
   - State whether your course is *recognized by* or *eligible for registration with* specific associations
   - If it isn't, be honest—and frame it as a complementary or independent modality

3. **Encourage students to do their homework**
   - Include links or guides to relevant associations
   - Teach them how to apply for insurance, register a business, or find legal terminology to describe their work

Bottom Line

You don't need to be government-accredited to offer powerful, transformative training—but you do need to understand:

- Where your course sits in the legal landscape
- What titles or claims are allowed
- What your students can realistically do with their certificate

Protect yourself. Protect your students. Teach with integrity.

When Do You Need a Teaching Credential?

This is one of the most misunderstood areas for aspiring educators and school founders—because the answer isn't always clear-cut.

Let's break it down:

What Is a Teaching Credential?

A teaching credential (or certificate/diploma in adult education) is a formal qualification that proves you've been trained to teach others—especially in a structured, classroom or institutional setting.

There are different types, such as:

- K–12 Teaching Certification – Required to teach in public elementary, middle, and high schools
- Post-Secondary Instructor Certificates – Often required to teach at colleges or government-accredited institutions
- Adult Education Diplomas – Valuable (and sometimes required) for teaching adults in vocational or continuing education settings
- Instructional Design or Train-the-Trainer Programs – Ideal for course creators, especially in the private sector

When You Don't Need One

If you are teaching:

- Your own method or modality
- In a private, unregulated school (e.g., Reiki training, breathwork certification, business coaching)
- On your own platform, in-person or online
- Workshops, retreats, short courses not tied to government funding or regulated professions

You do not legally need a credential to teach—though having one can boost your credibility, teaching skills, and student trust.

When You Do Need One

You'll usually need a formal credential if:

- You want to teach at a public or accredited post-secondary institution (college, university, trade school)
- Your program is tied to government funding or student loans
- You're applying for private career training institution designation (e.g., in BC, Alberta, or Ontario)
- Your province/state requires it to register as a vocational instructor
- You're teaching in a regulated profession where your school must follow association-approved standards

Some provinces (e.g., BC) require that at least one instructor in a career college holds a provincial Instructor Diploma to maintain accreditation.

Example:

You create a 40-hour course on holistic skincare techniques, and teach it under your licensed business.
You do *not* need a formal credential.

You apply to teach that same course as part of a certified esthetics program under an accredited college.
You'll likely need a teaching credential.

Bonus: Why It's Still Worth Getting One

Even if it's not required, an Adult Education Diploma or Instructor Certificate can:

- Help you design better learning experiences
- Improve student engagement and results
- Allow you to train other instructors under your brand
- Make you eligible for government funding, school partnerships, or accreditation
- Give you more freedom to grow and legitimize your school

Bottom Line:

You don't need a credential to teach. But you might need one to grow.

If your dream is to scale, register as a training institution, or reach a broader audience, getting formal instructor training is one of the best investments you can make.

Teacher Contracts & Intellectual Property Clauses: Protecting Your School and Your Content

When hiring teachers—whether contractors or employees—you must be crystal clear about who owns what, what happens if someone leaves, and how your curriculum is protected. These are the types of issues that can make or break your school's reputation, especially if students are left in limbo or your courses walk out the door.

Below are the key contract components every school owner should understand and implement.

1. Intellectual Property (IP): Who Owns the Course?

This is the most important clause in your contract. If a teacher develops new content while working for your school, you must clarify:

- Does your school own the course?
- Does the teacher retain ownership and simply license it to you?
- Can you keep offering the course if the teacher leaves?

Best Practice: All curriculum created under your employment or contract should be stated as "work for hire" or assigned to the school unless otherwise agreed upon.

Include this in writing:

"All intellectual property, including course content, manuals, videos, and materials developed during the period of instruction, shall remain the sole property of [School Name], unless otherwise specified in writing."

2. Non-Compete and Non-Solicitation Clauses

These clauses protect your business by setting boundaries around what a teacher can do during and after their time with you.

- Non-compete: Prevents a teacher from offering similar courses or starting a competing school within a certain distance and time frame after leaving.
    - Example: "The contractor agrees not to teach or offer similar training programs within 50 km for a period of 12 months following termination."
- Non-solicitation: Prevents a teacher from poaching students, staff, or using your client lists.
    - Example: "Instructor shall not solicit or enroll current or former students of [School Name] into private or competing training programs for a period of 18 months after termination."

Note: These clauses must be reasonable to hold up in court. Too broad or restrictive = unenforceable.

3. Teacher Leaves Mid-Program: What Happens Next?

Without proper planning, this can leave your students—and your reputation—in chaos.

Include clauses that address:

- **Notice Period**: Require a minimum number of weeks' notice before resignation or termination (e.g., 30 days).
- **Content Handover**: Teacher must leave all materials, assignments, grading, and course outlines to ensure another instructor can step in.
- **Transition Plan**: Outline your right to assign a replacement instructor and how the teacher must cooperate in the transition.

Sample clause:
"In the event of early termination by the instructor, they agree to provide all course documentation, student evaluations, and remaining teaching materials to ensure continuity of the program."

Why This Matters

If your school becomes accredited or regulated, you must demonstrate control and continuity of your programs. Letting teachers retain course ownership or leave mid-program without structure can:

- Jeopardize your registration
- Invalidate student certifications
- Damage your credibility
- Create refund liabilities

4. Protect Your Students—and Your School

When a teacher walks out the door, your course shouldn't go with them. And your students shouldn't pay the price.

Build teacher agreements that:

> Clearly assign intellectual property
> Prevent unfair competition
> Prioritize student outcomes
> Ensure course continuity

Is Government Accreditation Necessary?

Pros and Cons for School Owners

One of the biggest questions you'll face as a school founder is:

"Should I get government accreditation?"

And the honest answer is: It depends.

You can absolutely build a legitimate, profitable, and respected school **without** government accreditation. But you should fully understand what accreditation *is*, what it *does*, and what it *costs you*—in both time and freedom.

What Is Government Accreditation?

In most provinces, states, or countries, accreditation means that your school is:

- Registered with a government agency or regulatory body
- Monitored for quality, outcomes, instructor credentials, and student satisfaction
- Eligible for things like:
  - Government funding or student aid
  - Employer recognition
  - Public trust

In Canada, this is usually managed by provincial bodies like:

- Private Training Institutions Branch (PTIB) in British Columbia

- Advanced Education divisions in Alberta, Ontario, etc.

Pros of Government Accreditation

- Legitimacy & Credibility
  You can use terms like "recognized," "certified institution," and appeal to skeptical students or employers.
- Access to Government Funding
  Students may qualify for grants or loans, allowing you to reach those who couldn't otherwise afford training.
- Work with Regulated Professions
  Some designations require accredited education to count toward licensing (e.g., esthetics, massage therapy, health care assistants).
- More Institutional Opportunities
  Accreditation opens doors to being listed on official directories, partnering with colleges, or even offering international student visas.

Cons of Government Accreditation

- Strict Requirements
  You must meet and maintain curriculum standards, instructor credentials, business practices, and administrative processes.
- High Startup and Operating Costs
  Application fees, inspection fees, curriculum approvals, audited financials, annual reporting—it adds up.
- Loss of Flexibility
  You may not be able to pivot your curriculum quickly, change course content freely, or accept all instructors (even if experienced).
- Administrative Overhead
  Expect significant paperwork: student contracts, refund

policies, grading systems, instructor evaluations, and compliance tracking.

- ## Ongoing Audits
  You'll be subject to regular government reviews—and can be penalized, suspended, or shut down for non-compliance.

Who Is Accreditation For?

You may *want* to pursue accreditation if:

- Your program is part of a regulated industry
- Your students need recognized credentials
- You're ready to build a long-term institution
- You have access to capital and admin support

You may *skip* it if:

- You teach in unregulated fields (Reiki, coaching, wellness, business, creative arts)
- You want to retain control and agility
- You're serving students who care more about transformation than titles
- You're just starting and want to validate your model first

Bottom Line:

Government accreditation is powerful, but it's not always necessary.

If your students need access to financial aid, licensing, or employer-approved credentials, it may be the right next step. If you're an independent teacher building a heart-led school, you can do incredible work without it—as long as you stay ethical, transparent, and student-focused.

CANADA

In **British Columbia**, private career training institutions are regulated by the **Private Training Institutions Branch (PTIB)**, which falls under the **Ministry of Post-Secondary Education and Future Skills**. PTIB oversees institutions offering career-related programs longer than 40 hours or costing more than $4,000. Website: https://www.privatetraininginstitutions.gov.bc.ca

In **Alberta**, oversight of both public and private post-secondary institutions falls under the **Ministry of Advanced Education**. The relevant legislation is the **Post-secondary Learning Act**. More information can be found at: https://www.alberta.ca/advanced-education.aspx

Saskatchewan regulates its private vocational schools through the **Training Institutions Branch** under **Saskatchewan Advanced Education**. These schools are governed by the **Private Vocational Schools Regulation Act**. Learn more at: https://www.saskatchewan.ca/government/government-structure/ministries/advanced-education

In **Manitoba**, regulation of private vocational institutions falls under the **Department of Advanced Education, Skills and Immigration**. Details can be found at: https://www.gov.mb.ca/wd/ites/tes/index.html

Ontario's private career colleges are regulated by the **Ministry of Colleges and Universities** under the **Career Colleges Act, 2005**. Schools must be registered and programs approved. Website: https://www.ontario.ca/page/ministry-colleges-universities

In **Québec**, colleges (including private colleges and CÉGEPs) fall under the **Ministère de l'Enseignement supérieur**, and quality assurance is managed by the **Commission d'évaluation de l'enseignement collégial**. Website: https://www.quebec.ca/education/enseignement-superieur

New Brunswick oversees private career colleges through the **Department of Post-Secondary Education, Training and Labour,** which ensures compliance with the **Private Occupational Training Act.** Website: https://www2.gnb.ca/content/gnb/en/departments/post-secondary_education_training_and_labour.html

In **Nova Scotia,** private career colleges are regulated by the **Department of Labour and Advanced Education,** specifically under the **Private Career Colleges Division.** Visit: https://novascotia.ca/lae/privatecareercolleges

Newfoundland and Labrador manages its private training institutions through the **Department of Immigration, Population Growth and Skills,** under the **Private Training Regulations.** Website: https://www.gov.nl.ca/ipgs

On **Prince Edward Island,** private training is overseen by the **Department of Education and Lifelong Learning,** which ensures compliance with provincial training standards. Website: https://www.princeedwardisland.ca/en/topic/post-secondary-education

In the **Northwest Territories,** oversight of career and apprenticeship training is managed by the **Department of Education, Culture and Employment.** Website: https://www.ece.gov.nt.ca

Yukon has career training and apprenticeship programs administered through the **Department of Education.** More at: https://yukon.ca/en/education-and-schools

And in **Nunavut,** vocational training is generally facilitated through **Nunavut Arctic College,** with support from the **Department of Education.** Information: https://www.gov.nu.ca/education

USA

Federal Context

While accreditation (through U.S. Department of Education–recognized bodies) is handled at a national level, individual state approval or licensing is mandatory in every state for schools offering diplomas, certificates, or vocational. These state agencies authorize institutions to operate legally, confirm consumer protections, and are separate from accreditation.

Examples of State Authorizing Bodies

- In California, the Bureau for Private Postsecondary Education (BPPE) under the Department of Consumer Affairs licenses and monitors schools that offer certificates, diplomas, or vocational training.

- In New York, the Bureau of Proprietary School Supervision (BPSS)—a branch of the State Education Department—oversees non-degree, for-profit colleges and vocational schools .

- Oregon requires private career/trade institutions to be licensed through the Higher Education Coordinating Commission (HECC), specifically via its Private Career Schools Licensing unit .

- Washington State uses its Workforce Training & Education Coordinating Board (Governor-appointed) to license and regulate over 300 private career schools .

- In Ohio, the State Board of Career Colleges and Schools explicitly regulates private career colleges, ensuring they meet training standards .

- Illinois's **Board of Higher Education (IBHE)** governs business and vocational school approval under the Division of Private Business & Vocational Schools.
- In **Georgia**, the **Georgia Nonpublic Postsecondary Education Commission (GNPEC)** licenses any in-state or out-of-state institution that wants to use the terms "college" or "university".
- **Maryland** establishes policies and approves all postsecondary and career schools via the **Maryland Higher Education Commission**.

Untied Kingdom

Office for Students (OfS) — England's Higher-Education Regulator

Under the *Higher Education and Research Act 2017*, the **OfS** oversees universities and higher-education providers in England. It manages registration, ensures quality, and controls access to student loans and sponsorship for international students.

Quality Assurance Agency (QAA) — Quality for Higher Education

The **QAA** is the UK's independent quality body for universities and degree-awarding institutions. It sets and maintains standards, reviews, and advises on degree-awarding powers and educational quality.

Ofqual — Regulator for Qualifications (England)

The Office of Qualifications & Examinations Regulation (Ofqual) regulates GCSEs, A-Levels, vocational qualifications, and apprenticeships in England. It ensures certification levels correspond to the Regulated Qualifications Framework (RQF).

Ofsted — Regulates Early Years, Schools & Further Education

The Office for Standards in Education (Ofsted) inspects schools, colleges, teacher training, and childcare services in England, ensuring quality and compliance with education and skills standards.

Independent Schools Inspectorate (ISI) — Private School Evaluation

The ISI inspects private (independent) schools in England under government-approved standards. ISI also checks quality for independent further-education and English-language colleges, especially those with international students.

British Accreditation Council (BAC) — Global Private College Accreditation

The BAC accredits independent colleges and further-education institutions in the UK and abroad. It's recognized for institutions teaching international and non-EFL students and offers quality assurance through inspection and membership.

Ireland

- SOLAS: Government authority responsible for Further Education and Training (FET), including apprenticeships and PLCs, under the Department of Further and Higher Education.

- Quality and Qualifications Ireland (QQI): National agency managing the National Framework of Qualifications (NFQ), accrediting and quality-assuring further and higher education programs.
- Education and Training Boards (ETBs): 16 statutory regional bodies delivering and overseeing FET programs and apprenticeships.
  Together, SOLAS, QQI, and ETBs form a coordinated structure ensuring quality and accreditation.

Australia

AU National Regulators

Australian Skills Quality Authority (ASQA)

- ASQA is the national regulator for most Registered Training Organisations (RTOs).
- It operates under the *National Vocational Education and Training Regulator Act 2011*, registering and monitoring RTOs that offer VET qualifications like certificates, diplomas, and skill sets. ASQA also approves CRICOS registrations for international students.

Australian Qualifications Framework (AQF)

- The AQF sets the national standards for qualifications (Certificate I–IV, Diploma, Bachelor's, Master's, Doctorate).
- Providers must align their courses with AQF levels to issue officially recognized credentials.

State & Territory Regulators

Two states retain their own regulators for domestic VET providers:

- **Victoria** – *Victorian Registration and Qualifications Authority (VRQA)* regulates RTOs that serve only domestic students (unless under ASQA purview).
- **Western Australia** – *Training Accreditation Council (TAC)* in WA performs a similar role for domestic apprenticeships and RTOs.

All other states and territories—such as NSW, QLD, SA, TAS, ACT, NT—fall under ASQA regulation for VET.

TAFE and Apprenticeships

Technical and Further Education (TAFE)

institutions operate under state governments but are registered RTOs governed by ASQA (or VRQA/TAC in specific states). They deliver AQF-aligned qualifications integrated with apprenticeship frameworks.

Australian Apprenticeships

- Apprenticeships combine on-the-job training with structured off-the-job RTO learning.
- They are supported jointly by the federal Department of Employment and Workplace Relations (DEWR) and state/territory agencies.

Summary Table

Feature	Regulator(s)
RTO registration/program delivery (most states)	ASQA
RTOs in VIC (domestic)	VRQA
RTOs in WA (domestic)	Training Accreditation Council (TAC)
Qualification standards (AQF)	Australian Qualifications Framework
Apprenticeship management	DEWR + state/Territory Apprenticeship Units
Degree-level accreditation	Tertiary Education Quality and Standards Agency (TEQSA) – separate topic

New Zealand

- **New Zealand Qualifications Authority (NZQA):** Government crown entity overseeing the **New Zealand Qualifications Framework (NZQF)**, quality assurance of non-university tertiary providers, and regulation of apprenticeships and micro-credentials .
- **Tertiary Education Commission (TEC):** Crown agency directing tertiary education policy and funding for universities, polytechnics, and apprenticeship programs .
  NZQA manages the quality of qualifications and providers, while the TEC allocates funding and strategic direction.

Africa

South Africa

- **South African Qualifications Authority (SAQA)** is the statutory body that governs the **National Qualifications Framework (NQF)**, accredits qualifications, and recognizes professional bodies .
- **Department of Higher Education & Training (DHET)** oversees universities, public and private TVET colleges (formerly FET colleges), and combats unregistered "bogus" institutions.
- **Education and Training Quality Assurance (ETQA)** councils ensure quality standards in vocational education.

- Sector Education & Training Authorities (SETAs) manage learnerships, skills programmes, and workplace training across industries .

Kenya

- Kenya National Qualifications Authority (KNQA) manages the Kenya National Qualifications Framework (KNQF). It coordinates qualifications across formal, non-formal, and informal education sectors.
- Technical and Vocational Education and Training Authority (TVETA) licenses and accredits TVET institutions, trainers, and programs under the TVET Act .
- Commission for University Education (CUE) oversees accrediting degree-granting institutions and university programmes .

Other English-speaking countries (e.g., Nigeria, Ghana, Uganda)

Regulated training and professional education are managed by national councils, generally including:

- Councils for Medicine, Nursing, Engineering, Law, Accounting, and Architecture.
- NQF or Qualifications Authority frameworks that regulate vocational and academic qualifications.

Regulation levels vary, but if you're planning accredited certificate or diploma programs, these are the likely bodies involved.

Chapter 9: Insurance & Licensing for You and Your Students

Insurance Requirements for Schools: Beyond Basic Liability

When launching a private training school—whether online, in-person, or hybrid—insurance isn't just a checkbox. It's a vital part of protecting your reputation, your students, and your livelihood. Most new school owners know they need *commercial liability insurance*, but that's just the beginning. Depending on your setup and offerings, additional layers of protection may be necessary.

1. Commercial General Liability Insurance (CGL) – The Minimum

This covers:

- Third-party bodily injury (e.g., a student slips in your classroom)
- Property damage (e.g., you accidentally damage a rented venue)
- Legal defense costs if you're sued

Tip: Ensure your policy includes product liability if you sell kits, tools, or course materials.

2. Errors and Omissions Insurance (E&O) – Also Called Professional Liability

This covers mistakes, negligence, or misinformation related to the professional services you provide—like teaching.

Examples:

- A student claims they were taught outdated or harmful techniques
- You're accused of issuing a certificate fraudulently or without sufficient training
- A student sues after not being able to get insured or licensed based on your certification

Why It Matters: E&O protects you from the financial fallout of "teaching gone wrong," even if the claim is baseless.

3. Cybersecurity & Data Breach Insurance

Especially critical for online schools or hybrid models, where you collect and store:

- Student identification
- Payment information
- Transcripts and certificates
- Health data (if offering wellness/spa programs)

This insurance covers:

- Costs of notifying students about a breach
- Legal defense
- Credit monitoring services

- Data recovery and repair costs

Bonus: It can also cover cyber extortion (ransomware attacks) and lawsuits from compromised third-party platforms.

4. Contents and Equipment Insurance

If you have a physical school:

- Protect computers, classroom tech, spa/massage equipment, office furniture
- Covers damage from fire, theft, flood, vandalism, etc.

If you operate from home: Ensure your business contents are not excluded under your personal home policy.

5. Student Insurance (Optional but Wise)

If your students are:

- Practicing on the public (e.g., in massage, aesthetics, tattooing)
- Working off-site (e.g., internships, mobile spas)
  You might be required—or strongly advised—to provide student liability coverage or have them purchase it through an association or insurance provider.

6. Business Interruption Insurance

Covers income loss if your business is forced to close temporarily due to:

- Natural disaster
- Pandemic
- Fire
- Utility failure

Example: If your school must shut down for 3 weeks, this coverage can help pay ongoing expenses (rent, payroll, etc.).

7. Instructor-Specific Coverage

There's a difference between coverage for the institution and for individual instructors:

- Independent contractors should carry their own liability and E&O coverage
- If instructors are employees, ensure your policy covers their actions while teaching under your brand
- You may need to list instructors by name or add them as "insured parties" on your policy

Important: If a teacher teaches their own course under your school, and something goes wrong—they could sue *you* or *you could sue them* depending on what's covered.

Instructor Liability: What You Must Know

Becoming a teacher doesn't just mean sharing your knowledge—it means protecting yourself while doing it.

Teaching Comes with Risk

Whether you're teaching esthetics, energy healing, massage, or business development, you are:

- Giving advice
- Guiding physical practices
- Potentially impacting someone's health, income, or emotional state

That means you carry liability—and so does your business.

What Is Instructor Liability Insurance?

Instructor liability insurance (sometimes called educator's insurance or professional liability) protects you if a student or client:

- Claims your instruction caused them harm
- Accuses you of negligence or misinformation
- Experiences injury in your class or clinic

It typically covers:

- Legal defense costs
- Settlements or damages
- Professional errors or omissions
- Injuries during supervised practicals

When Do You Need It?

If you:

- Teach any hands-on course (massage, facial, PMU, Reiki, yoga, etc.)
- Offer certificates or diplomas
- Allow students to practice on others
- Rent a space for in-person learning
- Work with clients in front of students

Then yes—you need it.

Even if your students sign waivers, those don't always hold up in court. Insurance is your safety net.

Types of Instructor Coverage

- **Individual Educator's Policy** – Covers *you* as a teacher, even if you teach at multiple locations.
- **Business or School Policy** – Covers the *entity* (academy, training center), often includes student and visitor coverage.
- **General Liability** – For slips, trips, falls on your premises.
- **Professional Liability (E&O)** – For claims based on what you taught or advised.

Final Tip:

Talk to an insurance broker who specializes in education or wellness businesses. Describe exactly what you teach, where, how, and to whom. The wrong coverage—or lack of it—can mean a denied claim just when you need it most.

"You're not just a practitioner anymore. You're responsible for the actions of your students—especially during training."

What Your Students Need to Get Insurance and a Business Licence

Once a student completes your course, they often want to start working—either on clients or building a business. But here's the reality:

No matter how skilled they are, without proper documentation and clarity, they can't legally or safely operate.

Let's break it down into what your students need and how your course impacts that:

Getting Liability Insurance

For your student to get professional liability insurance, they usually need:

1. A certificate of completion or diploma
   o Must clearly state the course topic and completion date
   o Should be issued by a business with a valid business licence
   o Some insurers require the course provider (you) to have instructor credentials or experience
2. Course outline or syllabus
   o Some insurers ask to see what was covered in the training
3. Proof of hands-on training or case studies
   o Especially for services that involve touching clients (massage, PMU, esthetics, Reiki)

4. Proof that your training aligns with unregulated or lightly regulated sectors
   o If the modality is unregulated (like Reiki or body wraps), insurers will rely on your course credibility and your student's scope of practice

Tip: Encourage your students to keep a binder (digital or printed) with their certificate, outline, and proof of practice. It helps with claims and insurance applications.

Getting a Business Licence

A business licence is issued by the city or municipality. Each one has different rules, but most require:

1. A certificate or diploma showing they've been trained
2. Description of the service being offered
   o The city wants to ensure the service is legal and not a regulated health procedure
3. Proof of insurance
4. Zoning approval for their workspace (home or commercial)
5. Fire inspection or safety compliance (depending on the city and the services offered)

Your Role as the Educator

Your course needs to:

- Be well-structured and professionally presented

- Include clearly written learning outcomes and service descriptions
- Align with non-regulated or self-regulated practices in your country/province/state

When you provide quality training, documentation, and guidance, your students can confidently:

- Apply for insurance
- Apply for a business licence
- Open a practice or studio

When Students *Cannot* Legally Get a Licence

(...and what that means for you as their teacher)

It's a common—and risky—misunderstanding:

"If I take this course, I can start a business right away."

That's not always true.

Sometimes, students cannot get a business licence or insurance, even after completing your course. And if you're the educator, it's your responsibility to make this crystal clear upfront.

Common Reasons a Student Can't Get a Licence or Insurance

1. The service is regulated

- o Massage therapy, acupuncture, esthetics, and other modalities are regulated in some provinces/states.
- o If the training doesn't meet the governing body's standards or isn't recognized, students cannot legally offer that service—even with a certificate from you.

2. The course uses a protected title

- o Words like "Doctor," "Massage Therapist," or "Psychotherapist" are protected by law in many regions.
- o If your training uses these titles, your student may be blocked from licensing—or worse, accused of misrepresentation.

3. You are not recognized as a training provider

- o Some associations or insurers only accept certificates from accredited institutions or approved trainers.
- o If you're teaching independently, your student may struggle to get insurance unless your course is designed within the guidelines of unregulated practice.

4. The city doesn't recognize the service

- o Some cities simply do not license certain services (e.g., intuitive reading, energy work, spiritual coaching).
- o This doesn't mean it's illegal—but they may categorize it as *unlicensed*, or lump it under retail, coaching, or consulting.

What You Can Do About It

As a responsible course creator:

- Do your research for each area you intend to market to.
- Clearly state whether your course leads to unregulated, self-regulated, or government-regulated practice.
- Avoid titles that imply a regulated status if it doesn't apply.
- Provide insurance-friendly documentation, like syllabi, client safety practices, and ethical guidelines.

"Just because something is legal to teach doesn't mean the student can legally offer it as a service."

Real-World Example

Let's say your student finishes a 60-hour massage course with you. They want to open a studio in British Columbia, Canada.

Here's the issue:

Massage Therapy is regulated in BC under the CMTBC (College of Massage Therapists of BC). To legally offer massage, a person must graduate from a 2,200-hour approved school and pass board exams.

Your student? Not eligible. They cannot legally call themselves a massage therapist or offer massage services. But they *can* offer:

- Body treatments (e.g., wraps, exfoliation)
- Relaxation services (e.g., Reiki, guided breathwork, aromatherapy)

With a proper description and the right insurance, they could operate within the unregulated wellness space—but not under the title "massage therapist."

Working with Associations (or Creating Your Own Standards)

Once you begin teaching others, especially in specialized or emerging fields, you'll quickly encounter this question:

"Is your course recognized by an association?"

For many students (and insurers), an association equals credibility. But here's the truth: Not all associations are created equal—and not all industries have one.

Let's explore your options.

Why Work with an Association?

Associations often:

- Provide standardized curriculum guidelines
- Offer membership for practitioners
- Help students get insurance
- Set ethical codes and scope of practice
- Maintain public credibility and accountability

If you teach something like esthetics, aromatherapy, reflexology, Reiki, or coaching, partnering with an existing professional association can add serious legitimacy to your school.

How to Align with One

If you want your course to be "recognized":

1. Identify an active, credible association in your field.
2. Review their membership or school approval criteria—this may include instructor credentials, hours taught, hands-on requirements, curriculum topics, and ethics.
3. Apply for course recognition—some charge a fee, others ask for case studies or proof of outcomes.
4. If accepted, students can often mention they "trained with an [association-recognized school]," making it easier to get insurance and client trust.

Pro tip: Some associations offer a *school or educator membership tier.*

What If There's No Association?

If you're in a newer field—or your methods don't quite fit mainstream categories—you have two options:

1. Join an umbrella association

These broad organizations cover various wellness modalities. Examples:

- Natural Health Practitioners of Canada (NHPC)
- Canadian Examining Board of Health Care Practitioners
- International Practitioners of Holistic Medicine (IPHM)
- Complementary Medical Association (CMA)

They often accept self-designed programs as long as your teaching meets their baseline standards.

2. *Create your own framework*

If no suitable association exists, consider building:

- A code of ethics for your modality
- Scope of practice guidelines
- Continuing education pathways
- A directory of certified practitioners
- Optional membership tiers (student, certified, mentor)

Over time, this becomes its own *recognized standard*—especially if your graduates succeed, are insurable, and uphold client safety.

Creating Your Own Framework (When No Association Exists)

If your modality is new, niche, or just doesn't fit into existing associations, that doesn't mean you're stuck.

You *can* create your own credible, insurable, and respected standard—from scratch.

In fact, many of the largest associations in the wellness and healing fields began this exact way:
A trusted practitioner developed a clear system, trained others with integrity, and structured it into a professional community.

Here's how to do it:

1. Develop a Code of Ethics

A clear code of ethics is the foundation of any respected profession.

It shows clients, students, and insurers that your practitioners are held to a standard of integrity and conduct.

Include principles such as:

- Do no harm (physical, emotional, energetic)
- Informed consent before treatment or training
- Confidentiality and privacy
- Scope of competence (only practice what you're trained in)
- Respect for client autonomy and belief systems
- No diagnosis or medical claims unless qualified to do so

Make this document part of your course manual and student onboarding. Require signed acknowledgment.

2. Define Scope of Practice

Scope of practice is what your graduates *can and cannot* do.

This protects:

- The student from overstepping legal boundaries
- The client from misunderstanding what's being offered
- You from liability and misrepresentation

For example, a Reiki practitioner may:
Offer energetic balancing
Not diagnose illness or prescribe medication

A body wrap technician may:
Apply products for cosmetic body treatments
Not promise weight loss, cure cellulite, or manipulate lymph nodes

Write this out clearly and include disclaimers students can use in their own marketing and consent forms.

3. Offer Continuing Education Pathways

Create a tiered system that encourages professional growth and keeps your modality evolving.

Examples:

- Level 1: Foundational Training
- Level 2: Advanced Applications
- Level 3: Teacher or Mentor Certification
- Specialty Add-Ons: Ethics, Trauma-Informed Care, Case Studies, Business Development

Offering continuing education not only supports your graduates— it reinforces your authority as a leading voice in the field.

4. Maintain a Directory of Certified Practitioners

This gives your modality external visibility and supports your students' credibility.

Build a page on your website listing:

- Certified name
- Location or online availability
- Level of training
- Optional photo, bio, or contact

Bonus:

- Add a search filter (by country, service, specialty)
- Issue digital badges or certificates they can link to

You're building a *community*, not just a course.

5. Create Membership Tiers

Let your students stay connected and advance through your system. This might include:

- Student Member: In training
- Certified Practitioner: Completed core training and passed assessment
- Advanced/Level 2 Practitioner: Completed additional modules or mentorship
- Mentor or Trainer: Can guide others or teach with your framework

Add benefits such as:

- Member-only resources
- Case study templates
- Practice-building workshops
- Marketing support
- Listing in your directory
- CEU tracking (if you decide to offer CE credits)

You become more than a teacher—you become a governing body, and your brand becomes the recognized authority in that niche.

Real-Life Example

Think of modalities like:

- BodyTalk
- ThetaHealing
- Emotion Code
- Access Bars
- Touch for Health

Each started with a person who codified a healing approach, taught it responsibly, and structured it with ethical and educational standards.

You can do the same.

Remember

- Associations don't grant legal authority—but they bridge the gap between training and practice in unregulated sectors.
- Whether you align with one or build your own, the goal is the same: Protect the public, support your students, and elevate your credibility.

Part 3: Running & Growing Your Private Training School

Chapter 10: Setting Up the School Space

Renting vs. Home-Based vs. Shared Space

Your school doesn't need to be huge, fancy, or located in a corporate building to be real. In fact, some of the most successful alternative education programs started from a home office, a shared treatment room, or a rented back room in someone else's business.

The key isn't **where** you teach—it's **how** you set up your space for professionalism, safety, and compliance.

Let's break down your three main options:

1. Home-Based School

Pros:

- Lowest cost
- Full control over your schedule
- No commute
- Comfortable, welcoming environment

Cons:

- Zoning restrictions (some cities may not allow in-home businesses)
- Parking and accessibility issues
- Limited space for larger groups or equipment
- Harder to separate personal and professional boundaries

Key Considerations:

- Apply for a *home-based business licence* with your municipality
- Designate a specific area for teaching (e.g., a treatment room, converted basement)
- Be mindful of signage rules (many cities limit signs in residential areas)
- Ensure safety features are in place: fire extinguisher, exits, and insurance for visitors
- Have students sign clear liability and behavior agreements when entering your home

Many holistic schools—especially Reiki, coaching, and bodywork— successfully operate from home with the right setup.

2. Shared or Rented Space

This includes:

- Renting by the hour in a wellness center
- Using a backroom in a spa, yoga studio, or coworking space
- Partnering with another practitioner or teacher to split a lease

Pros:

- More professional environment
- Shared resources (tables, chairs, linens)
- Flexible commitment (hourly or day rates)
- Often comes with built-in exposure to clients or students

Cons:

- You may not have control over decor, availability, or layout
- You'll need to coordinate schedules carefully
- May not feel "fully yours," which can limit branding

Key Considerations:

- Ensure you're allowed to *teach* in the space, not just see clients
- Check what insurance covers—you may need your own
- Sign a written agreement clarifying use, responsibilities, and expectations
- Make sure the space meets fire and occupancy codes if you're bringing in multiple students

3. Leased or Commercial Space

This is the most "official" route and allows you to operate like a formal school or academy.

Pros:

- Full control over branding, scheduling, signage, and renovations
- Easier to get approved for zoning, fire, and occupancy
- Room to expand and host larger groups
- Adds instant credibility

Cons:

- Higher overhead (rent, utilities, business taxes)
- Long-term lease commitments
- More regulation (ADA accessibility, inspections, permits)

Key Considerations:

- Apply for the proper zoning permit before signing a lease
- Schedule a fire inspection and ensure exits, alarms, extinguishers, and signage meet code
- Budget for start-up costs like desks, signage, lighting, insurance, security deposits
- Choose a location that is accessible by public transport or has nearby parking

You don't need a 10,000 sq. ft. campus. My first "school" was just over 1,000 sq. ft.—but I had fire approval, liability insurance, and a heart full of purpose. That made it official.

Required Equipment and Legal Considerations

Whether you're teaching energy healing, spa treatments, coaching, or theory-based classes, there are non-negotiable essentials that turn your space from casual to credible — and keep you compliant with local laws.

This applies whether you're running your school from home, in a shared studio, or in a commercial facility.

Basic Physical Equipment (Every School Needs These)

No matter your modality, your space should have:

- Chairs and writing surfaces (desks, tables, or clipboards)
- Adequate lighting (natural is great, but task lighting is a must)
- Power sources (accessible outlets for devices or projectors)
- Clock or timer (for timed exercises and assessments)
- Whiteboard or flip chart (or digital equivalent if online or hybrid)
- First aid kit (with clearly labeled emergency numbers)
- Trash and recycling bins
- Hand sanitizer / hand-washing station
- Storage for supplies, records, and course materials

Even in a minimalist or mobile setup, you should aim to look and operate like a *real* school — because you are one.

Modality-Specific Equipment (Based on What You Teach)

For bodywork or hands-on training:

- Massage or spa tables (with face cradles and sanitizable covers)
- Towels, sheets, bolsters, blankets
- Proper sanitation setup (gloves, disinfectants, hand soap)
- Sharps container (if using needles, PMU, or anything with skin penetration)
- Mirrors, sinks, fans, or humidifiers if needed for your service

For beauty or esthetics:

- Rolling trolleys
- Proper lighting/magnifiers
- Product storage with labeling
- Covered containers for disposables
- Machine compliance stickers (CSA/UL-approved if electric)

For energy work or lecture-based classes:

- Comfortable seating for meditative or quiet sessions
- Speaker system or calming music option
- Visual aids (chakra charts, anatomy posters, etc.)

Legal Considerations

1. Business Licence:

Must be active and reflect your true business type (e.g., private education, health coaching, consulting).

2. Fire Inspection:

Required if you'll have students in-person. You'll need:

- Two exits
- Fire extinguisher(s)
- Visible occupancy load sign (for group spaces)
- Smoke detectors and clear signage for exits

3. Zoning Compliance:

Check that your space is zoned for educational or instructional use. Some cities prohibit teaching in residential zones without special permits.

4. Accessibility (ADA or Equivalent):

While not always required for very small schools or home-based spaces, it's good practice to:

- Ensure wheelchair access
- Offer printed materials in larger fonts
- Have policies for inclusive learning (sensory-friendly environments, etc.)

5. Insurance Requirements:

You should carry:

- Commercial General Liability Insurance
- Instructor Liability Insurance
- Contents Coverage for theft or damage

- Possibly Errors & Omissions (E&O) if teaching high-stakes topics

6. Records Compliance:

You are legally responsible for:

- Safeguarding student contact details and payment info
- Storing signed intake/consent forms securely
- Offering receipts and student transcripts (if requested)
- Maintaining copies of certificates issued

Disability & Accessibility Compliance: Creating Inclusive Learning Spaces (Online and Off)

Whether you're teaching from your living room, a professional training centre, or an online platform, you are legally and ethically responsible for ensuring your school is accessible to students with disabilities.

Too often, accessibility is overlooked by small schools or solo educators—yet in Canada (and in many international contexts), accessibility isn't optional. It's a legal obligation under:

- The Accessible Canada Act
- The Canadian Charter of Rights and Freedoms
- Provincial Human Rights Codes (e.g., BC Human Rights Code, AODA in Ontario)

If your school is regulated, accessibility may also be a requirement for your license or accreditation.

A. Physical Accessibility for In-Person Schools

If you operate a brick-and-mortar school location, you must ensure your facilities are physically accessible to students with mobility or sensory challenges.

Requirements may include:

- Wheelchair-accessible entrances and ramps
- Wide hallways and doorways
- Accessible washrooms (grab bars, maneuvering space)
- Non-slip flooring
- Designated accessible parking spaces
- Clear signage and emergency exit plans

Even if your city zoning didn't require this when you first opened, you must provide reasonable accommodation under human rights law.

Tip: Conduct a physical accessibility audit before admitting students onsite.

B. Online Accessibility (Digital Compliance)

If your school includes online learning, your digital content and platforms must comply with the Web Content Accessibility Guidelines (WCAG 2.1) to accommodate users with:

- Visual impairments (blindness, low vision, color blindness)
- Hearing loss
- Cognitive or learning disabilities
- Mobility impairments (difficulty using a mouse or keyboard)

Key Accessibility Features to Include:

- Alt-text for all images
- Subtitles/captions for videos
- Readable fonts and high contrast
- Keyboard navigation
- Descriptive link text (not just "click here")
- Screen-reader compatibility
- Transcripts for video/audio files

Platforms like Thinkific, Teachable, Kajabi, and Podia are working to improve accessibility—but not all features are compliant out of the box. Review your platform settings and content carefully.

C. Legal Obligations by Region (Canada)

CA Federally:

- **Accessible Canada Act (ACA)** applies to federally regulated entities, but sets the gold standard for inclusion and digital equity.

Provincially:

- **AODA (Ontario)**: Mandatory for most businesses, including private training providers
- **BC Human Rights Code**: Requires equal access and reasonable accommodation
- **Other provinces** have similar codes requiring you to provide accessible services or justify why you cannot

Note: Even unregulated schools can face human rights complaints if accessibility is not offered.

D. Reasonable Accommodation vs. Undue Hardship

You must offer reasonable accommodations unless doing so would cause undue hardship. This means:

- You may be expected to move a class, adjust an assignment, or provide alternate formats.
- You are not expected to undertake renovations or tech overhauls that would bankrupt your business—but you must demonstrate that you considered options in good faith.

Why It Matters (Beyond Compliance)

Making your school accessible:

- Increases your potential student base
- Builds a reputation for inclusivity and professionalism
- Prevents human rights complaints
- Aligns your business with modern values and federal equity goals

Final Thought:

Start small—but start. Whether it's adding closed captions to your next video or offering an intake form that asks about accommodation needs, accessibility is a practice, not a checkbox. Build it into your business now, and your school will grow with integrity and resilience.

Long-Term Record Keeping: The 55-Year Requirement

If you're operating as a private vocational institution, college, or any post-secondary training program—even if it's unregulated—you may be required by your province, state, or governing body to retain student records for up to 55 years.

Yes, 55 years.

This ensures students (or employers, insurance companies, or regulatory bodies) can access their training credentials *decades later*.

It also demonstrates your commitment to educational integrity and accountability.

How Long Must You Keep Records

The required retention period depends on the province and whether your school is regulated or unregulated, but general best practices are:

- Transcripts & Diplomas: Minimum 55 years (especially for accredited or regulated institutions)
- Enrollment Contracts & Attendance: At least 7–10 years
- Financial Records (tuition payments, refunds): 6–7 years (CRA requirement)
- Medical or Health History Forms (for wellness/spa schools): 10 years after last visit, or longer if minor

Tip: Check with your provincial regulator (e.g., PTIB in BC) for the exact timeframes you're expected to meet.

What Records Must Be Kept?

Each student file should include:

- Full Legal Name (as used for certification)
- Date of Birth (if required by your licensing region)
- Copy of Course Registration (signed contract or enrollment form)
- Transcripts (grades, evaluations, attendance)
- Certificates and/or Diplomas Issued
- Copy of Signed Intake and Consent Forms

- Communication Record (important emails or notes regarding status, complaints, etc.)

Optional but helpful:

- Payment history/invoice copies
- Completed assignments or case study summaries
- Notes on disciplinary action, if any

Privacy Law Compliance (Canada)

In Canada, private training schools must comply with PIPEDA (Personal Information Protection and Electronic Documents Act) and any provincial privacy legislation. Key principles include:

- Informed Consent: Students must know why you're collecting their data and how it will be used.
- Limited Collection: Only gather what's necessary.
- Access Rights: Students can request to view or correct their data.
- Data Minimization: Avoid storing more than needed or longer than required.
- Breach Notification: You must notify the Privacy Commissioner and affected individuals if a breach occurs.

How to Store Records

You may store records digitally, physically, or both, but storage must comply with privacy legislation:

Digital Storage Must Be:

- Encrypted
- Password protected
- Backed up regularly
- Hosted on Canadian servers (to stay compliant with Canadian laws unless informed consent is obtained)
- Cloud services like Dropbox or Google Drive may not meet standards unless configured properly

Physical Records Must Be:

- Stored in a locked cabinet or room
- Access limited to authorized personnel
- Protected against fire, flood, or theft

Caution: Never leave contracts, student IDs, or medical info lying around in open classrooms or offices.

Digital Storage: A Modern Solution

Storing paper records for 55 years is not just impractical—it's risky. Fires, floods, and simple decay can wipe out decades of files.

Digital recordkeeping is now the standard, and there are companies that specialize in secure, long-term academic storage.

Example: Data Witness

www.**DataWitness**.com is a Canadian company that offers secure, legally admissible digital archiving. It's designed for institutions like yours.

Key benefits:

- Secure cloud-based storage
- Records are time-stamped and locked
- Accessible by government authorities if required
- You can retrieve records for student requests at any time
- Protects your institution in case of legal audits or licensing reviews

Pro Tip: Even if you close your school, your responsibility to provide records *doesn't end*. Services like Data Witness ensure you don't have to personally manage them forever.

Best Practices

- Create a digital Student File Template you use for every enrollee
- Organize folders by intake year, course, or certification level
- Store files in both a primary and redundant cloud location (or use a service like Data Witness that handles both)
- Establish a Records Request Procedure for alumni or verifications

By setting up your records system early—and keeping it clean— you not only protect your students' futures…
You protect your reputation.

Pro Tip: Before opening your doors, make a checklist and pretend an inspector is walking through. Ask:
"Would they see a safe, organized, and professional learning space?"

If the answer is yes, you're ready.

Homework, Written Exams & Hosting Practical Sessions

Teaching isn't just about presenting content — it's about guiding transformation. And that means evaluating how well your students are absorbing, applying, and embodying what you teach.

To maintain professionalism and credibility (especially if you're issuing certificates or diplomas), structured evaluation methods are essential.

Let's break it down.

Homework: How Much Is Enough?

Homework reinforces retention. It's especially valuable for adult learners who need time to reflect, review, and apply.

Best practices:

- ## Keep it purposeful – Homework should directly reinforce what was just taught.
- ## Avoid busywork – Quality over quantity. 1–3 meaningful questions or reflections are more effective than 10 disconnected tasks.
- ## Use formats that fit your modality:
    - o Journaling (for energy, coaching, wellness)
    - o Quizzes or fill-in-the-blank (for anatomy, theory)
    - o Client logs or case studies (for hands-on skills)
    - o Reflection questions or peer feedback (for growth-based training)

Tip: Always give clear instructions, due dates, and how it will be marked (pass/fail, completion, rubric, etc.)

Written Exams: When and Why

Written exams are useful for:

- Measuring understanding of theory, ethics, anatomy, contraindications, history, or scope of practice
- Demonstrating academic credibility (especially for insurance and professional use)

Structure of a professional exam:

- Multiple choice for retention
- Short answer for critical thinking
- Case scenario or "what would you do if…" for ethics and application
- Open book or closed book, depending on the level of mastery required

Legal consideration:

If your course is being used toward licensure or insurance, written exams show you held the student accountable for learning, not just attendance.

Hosting Practical Exams (Hands-On)

If your course includes physical application — massage, facials, PMU, energy work, lash extensions, etc. — you must evaluate their hands-on competency.

This protects:

- The **student** (to know they're ready)
- The **client** (to ensure safety)
- **You** (in case a certificate is challenged by an insurance provider or authority)

Practical Exam Must-Haves:

1. ## A rubric (grading sheet)
   Includes points for:
   - o Setup and hygiene
   - o Technique or skill accuracy
   - o Client communication and professionalism
   - o Cleanup and follow-through
   - o Confidence and flow of session
2. ## A model (real or mock)
   - o Live models are ideal, but mannequins or role-play can work in early levels
   - o Make sure models sign consent forms too
3. ## A clean, safe, legally compliant space
   - o Fire code, proper lighting, sanitized surfaces, handwashing stations
4. ## Evaluation by a qualified examiner
   - o This can be you, a co-instructor, or a pre-approved senior practitioner
   - o Examiners must **not coach or prompt during the test**
5. ## Clear pass/fail or grading criteria
   - o If the student fails, outline their options for remediation or retest

Additional Considerations:

- Video exams are acceptable when in-person isn't possible
    o Must include setup, treatment, and breakdown
    o Provide clear video submission guidelines
    o Store videos as part of the student's assessment record
- Retake policies should be written into your course terms
    o Example: 1 free retake, then $50 per additional attempt
    o Limit attempts to maintain standards (e.g., 2 or 3 max)

Final Tip

Document everything: scores, feedback, dates, and any accommodations or issues during exams. These records protect you, your student, and the legitimacy of your program.

Chapter 11: Enrollment, Marketing & Messaging

Setting Fair Tuition

Tuition pricing is one of the most important decisions you'll make as a school owner — and also one of the most emotionally charged.

Charge too little, and you undermine your credibility (and your income).
Charge too much without support, and you risk limiting access or facing skepticism.

The goal? Balance value, integrity, and sustainability.

What Is "Fair" Tuition?

Fair doesn't always mean "cheap." It means:

- Transparent: Students understand exactly what they're paying for

- **Competitive:** You've researched your niche and similar programs
- **Sustainable:** It covers your time, expertise, materials, and overhead
- **Equitable:** There's room for access (payment plans, scholarships, etc.)

Factors to Consider When Setting Tuition:

1. **Your expertise**
   Years of experience, credentials, and results add value — don't undersell them.

2. **Length of course**
   A 2-day workshop won't be priced like a 300-hour diploma program.

3. **Delivery format**
   o Online-only courses may be cheaper to offer (but not always to build!)
   o In-person or hybrid programs require space, equipment, and setup

4. **What's included**
   o Are materials provided? (Kits, books, oils, machines?)
   o Are case studies, mentorship, or follow-up support part of the price?
   o Will students walk away with certification they can *use* professionally?

5. **Regulatory standing**
   o If you're government-accredited or offer insurable training, that justifies higher tuition

6. **Market expectations**
   o What do students typically pay for comparable training in your field or region?
   o Are you offering more transformation or credibility than others?

Sample Tuition Benchmarks (2025 Estimates):

- 2–3 hour intro workshop (non-certification): $49–$97
- 1-day hands-on class (with take-home kit): $197–$497
- Multi-day certificate course (12–40 hrs): $500–$1,500
- Diploma program (100–600+ hrs): $2,000–$12,000+

Remember: You're not charging for *hours*—you're charging for outcomes.

Tools to Support Fair Tuition:

- Tiered pricing options: e.g., standard, VIP (with coaching), audit-only
- Early bird or launch discounts: for limited time enrollments
- Installment/payment plans: make it accessible without devaluing
- Bonus content or kits: increase perceived value without raising cost

Bottom Line

Your course pricing should:
Reflect the transformation offered
Sustain your school's operations
Build trust through transparency
Position you as a credible educator

Fair Tuition for International Students

As more schools expand their reach online, international students are becoming a key part of many programs—even those run from small, private institutions. But this raises an important question: What's considered "fair" tuition when you're teaching across borders?

Why This Matters

International students often face:

- Currency exchange challenges (what's affordable in one country may be expensive in another)
- Lack of access to student funding (loans or grants may not apply outside their home country)
- Higher costs for materials, shipping, or time zone differences
- Legal confusion about what their certificate or diploma means in their home region

What You Should Consider

1. Transparent pricing.
   Always list your full fees up front—tuition, materials, technology access, certificates, and any additional charges.

2. ## Currency conversion.
   If possible, list the equivalent in major currencies (e.g., USD, EUR, GBP) and let students know what payment methods you accept.

3. ## Tiered pricing models.
   Offer adjusted tuition for countries with lower average incomes, or create a scholarship program for international access.

4. ## Accessibility.
   Ensure that course delivery (time zones, access to recordings, English level, tech requirements) is realistic for students around the world.

5. ## Clarify recognition.
   Make sure your international students understand whether their certificate or diploma is:
   - o Educational only
   - o Recognized by any associations
   - o Valid for business licensing or insurance in their country

6. ## Refund policies.
   Include fair refund policies that account for different international banking timelines or potential delays in delivery.

Bottom Line:

Fair tuition isn't about charging everyone the same—it's about creating access and clarity while respecting the value of your education. When you approach international tuition with integrity and foresight, you expand your school's reach—and your impact.

International Student Tuition Policies in Canada

No Price Caps for International Students

- Domestic tuition increases are often regulated—for instance, in British Columbia, domestic university fees are capped at 2%.
- In contrast, international student tuition is unregulated in most provinces. This means schools and colleges can increase fees by any amount, or set them arbitrarily—leading to dramatic fee hikes over time.

How High Are the Fees?

- In BC, international tuition has soared since 2006:
  - Up 64% since 2006, and 594% since 1991.
- Nationally, undergraduate tuition averages over $40,000/year for international students (2024–25), with postgraduate rates also climbing.

Government Response & Rising Requirements

1. Higher Proof-of-Funds Requirements
   - Starting September 1, 2025, international applicants (excluding Québec) must demonstrate $22,895 CAD for living expenses alone—up from $20,635—on top of tuition.
2. Cap on Study Permits

- o The federal government has capped new study permits at about 437,000 per year, a 10% reduction from 2024, to control demand and housing strain

Why This Matters for Educators

- **Ethical Considerations**: Charging inflated fees without transparency risks exploiting international students, especially those unaware of domestic rate disparities.
- **Regulatory Shift**: Though not yet price-regulated, international tuition is under growing scrutiny—especially as public backlash increases.
- **Market Access**: Higher cost-of-living thresholds and permit caps may lead to fewer international students, impacting school finances.
- **Reputation Risk**: Schools seen to be taking advantage can face reputational damage and potential regulatory exposure in the future.

Best Practices for Fair Tuition

- Be **transparent**: Break down tuition, materials, fees, and currency rates.
- Monitor and **justify increases**: Keep them aligned with cost inflation, not market trends.
- Consider **differentiated models**: Offer tiered pricing or scholarship support for students from lower-income countries.
- Stay **aware of policy changes**—proof-of-funds rules and cap announcements matter.

Final Takeaway

Canada currently allows unlimited tuition pricing for international students—a system that has led to quadrupling fees compared to domestic levels . While not illegal, it's ethically and strategically important for school founders to review their pricing structures and ensure they remain fair, transparent, and sustainable— especially as governmental scrutiny and market shifts increase.

Clear Refund Policies And Contracts

Are non-negotiable when running a school — whether you're teaching online, in-person, or both.

They protect:

- You, from legal disputes or financial loss
- The student, by setting clear expectations
- Your school, by ensuring consistency and professionalism

Why You Need a Contract (Even for Short Courses)

A signed student agreement helps eliminate misunderstandings. It outlines:

- What's included in the course
- Tuition fees and what they cover
- Attendance, behavior, and academic expectations
- What happens if the student quits, is dismissed, or wants a refund

Pro Tip: Use plain language. Avoid legal jargon unless a lawyer is reviewing your document.

What to Include in a Student Contract

1. Full course details
   - Name of course, start/end dates, delivery format
   - Contact hours or access window (e.g., "6 months online access")
   - Certification conditions (case studies, exams, attendance, etc.)

2. ## Fees and payment terms
   - o Tuition total, what it includes
   - o Deposit amounts and due dates
   - o Installment plan breakdown (if offered)
3. ## Refund policy *(see below)*
4. ## Dismissal policy
   - o Reasons you may remove a student (misconduct, plagiarism, safety risks)
   - o What happens financially if they're removed
5. ## Student responsibilities
   - o Behavior, professionalism, confidentiality, respectful communication
6. ## Intellectual property
   - o Whether they can resell or reuse your course material
7. ## Signature & date

Refund Policies: How to Structure Them

There is no single law dictating refund policies for private education unless you are government-accredited. However, it's best practice to:

- Follow fair consumer guidelines
- Be clear and consistent
- Put policies in writing — *not just on your website, but in your contracts*

Sample Refund Structures

Option 1: Time-Based

- Full refund if canceled within 48–72 hours of purchase (before course begins)
- Partial refund (e.g., 50%) within the first 25% of the course
- No refund after 25% completion or access/download

Option 2: Access-Based (for online courses)

- Full refund if student hasn't accessed any lessons
- Partial refund if <25% accessed and within 7 days
- No refund after access to core materials (videos, manuals, kits)

Option 3: Deposit-Based (for in-person)

- The deposit is non-refundable
- Tuition minus deposit is refundable if notice is given 14+ days before the course
- No refund within 7 days of course start (unless special circumstances)

If offering government-accredited training, your refund policy must follow that province/state's education standards.

Keep in Mind:

- Always have the student sign the contract before the course starts
- Digitally timestamped consent (via software like DocuSign, JotForm, or Data Witness) counts
- Make a copy easily accessible to both you and the student

Marketing Compliance & Ethical Advertising for Private Training Schools

Creating a compelling message is vital to attracting students—but if your marketing overpromises or misleads, you could face serious consequences, especially as a training provider. Whether you're regulated or not, the following rules and best practices apply.

1. What You're Legally Allowed to Claim

You must be able to prove any claims you make. That includes:

- Job placement statistics:
  Only state percentages if you can back them up with records.
  Avoid generalizations like "98% of our students find jobs!" unless you've tracked and documented those results.
- Salary expectations:
  Say: "Past students have earned up to $X based on self-employment success stories."
  Don't say: "You'll make $80,000 a year as a reflexologist" unless you're quoting official labor data with citation.

- ## Certification recognition:
  Clarify: "Our certificate is recognized by [specific association] for liability insurance."
  Avoid: "You'll be fully licensed after graduation" if that's not true in your province/state.

2. Using the Word "Certified"

In Canada (and many other countries), the word *"certified"* can only be used under specific conditions:

- You may say:
  "Certificate of Completion" (if no licensing/accreditation is involved)
  "Certified by [Association Name]" (only if you've been approved and registered)
- Avoid misleading phrases like:
  "Government-certified school" if you're not regulated
  "Internationally Certified" unless you're backed by a legitimate global body

Legal Note: Using the wrong terminology can trigger consumer protection complaints—even lawsuits.

3. Testimonials and Reviews

- ## Must be real. Never use AI-generated or fake reviews.
- ## Must be verifiable. Keep student consent and written approval on file.
- ## Don't promise outcomes. Testimonials can share experiences, not guarantee results.

Example:
"This course helped me start my wellness practice."
"This course guarantees you'll get a six-figure income."

4. Anti-Spam Laws – CASL (Canada's Anti-Spam Legislation)

If you're sending emails to Canadians, you must:

- Get express consent (opt-in checkbox, not pre-checked)
- Include your business name and contact info
- Provide a working unsubscribe option in every email

Fines under CASL can reach $1 million+ per violation, even for small schools.

Tip: Use tools like MailerLite, ConvertKit, or ActiveCampaign, which offer built-in CASL-compliant features.

5. Transparency Builds Trust

Ethical advertising isn't just a legal requirement—it's also a competitive advantage. Today's learners are savvy. When you're clear about:

- What your course *can* do
- What it *won't* do
- And who it's *for* (and not for)...

...you build credibility, loyalty, and long-term success.

Building Trust: Your Bio, Reviews & Testimonials

When a student considers enrolling in your course, they're not just buying education — they're buying you.

They want to know:

- Can I trust this person?
- Are they qualified?
- Will I get real value?
- Have others had success?

That's where your bio, reviews, and testimonials do the heavy lifting. They build emotional and professional trust — the kind of trust that sells courses without pressure.

Your Bio: Write It to Connect, Not Impress

You don't need a Ph.D. or decades of teaching to be credible — but you do need to clearly explain why you're qualified to teach what you teach.

Your bio should include:

- Your background (education, experience, credentials)
- How you got into your field or method (personal story = connection)
- What makes your teaching unique (approach, tools, values)
- A warm, authentic tone — not a stiff résumé

Tip: Write it in first person if you want to sound approachable. Use third person if you want a more formal tone. Either works — just be consistent.

Example Bio (Conversational Style)

"I never planned on becoming a teacher, let alone running a school — but a zoning issue turned my healing practice into something much bigger. Since 1999, I've been helping others step into their calling through natural medicine, energy healing, and professional training. My background includes over 20 certifications, a doctorate in natural medicine, and decades of hands-on experience in both healing and business. My passion is helping others turn their wisdom into thriving careers — with integrity, confidence, and soul."

Reviews & Testimonials: Social Proof That Sells

Think of testimonials as word-of-mouth referrals in writing. They reassure potential students that:

- The course works
- You deliver on your promises
- They'll be supported throughout the process

You need at least 3–5 strong testimonials per course.

What Makes a Good Testimonial?

- Specificity: What problem did they have? What changed? What did they learn?
- Relatability: Future students should see themselves in the success story
- Outcome-focused: "I now have a successful practice" beats "It was nice"

How to Collect Testimonials (Ethically)

- Ask after a milestone: when a student completes the course, gets their first client, or launches their business
- Use a simple form: Include prompts like:
  - What was your biggest takeaway?
  - What would you say to someone considering this course?
  - How has this training helped you in real life?
- Get written permission to use their name, photo, or video
- Make it easy: Offer to draft a summary based on their words and get their approval

Where to Use Your Bio & Testimonials

- Website course pages
- Landing pages and ads
- Social media (in posts or Stories)
- Inside the course welcome modules
- In your email marketing funnels

Pro Tip: Create a "Student Success" or "Graduate Spotlight" feature — people love to read stories of real people doing what they dream of doing.

Handling Complaints & Student Disputes: Protecting Your School with Transparency & Process

Whether you're a one-person training academy or a multi-instructor private college, student complaints are inevitable—and how you handle them can make or break your credibility.

Especially for regulated schools, it's not just best practice—it's a legal requirement to have a formal dispute resolution policy. But even for unregulated or short-course programs, having a transparent, documented system helps you:

- Protect your school legally
- Resolve issues before they escalate
- Maintain your reputation and student trust

A. What Regulated Schools Are Required to Have

If your school is regulated (e.g., by PTIB in British Columbia, Career Colleges Ontario, or another provincial authority), you are legally obligated to:

- Develop and publish a clear *Dispute Resolution Policy*
- Make it available to students before enrollment
- Include it in the Student Enrollment Contract
- Provide a clear step-by-step process for resolving complaints

- Maintain a record of the complaint and outcome for audit purposes

The process must include:

1. **Attempted resolution with the instructor** or staff member involved
2. **Escalation to the school director or owner**
3. **Written formal complaint** (template often required)
4. **Resolution timeline** (typically 30 days)
5. Final step: advising students of their **right to contact the regulator** if unresolved

B. Templates & Internal Procedures

Even if you're not regulated, it's smart to have a **Complaint Handling Policy** in place. Here's what you'll want to include:

Sample Internal Complaint Procedure:

1. **Initial Conversation**: Encourage the student to speak with the instructor directly.
2. **Written Complaint**: If unresolved, ask the student to submit a written complaint (include date, issue, what resolution they're seeking).
3. **Internal Review**: Director/owner reviews and responds within 10–30 business days.
4. **Resolution & Documentation**: Response is sent to the student in writing and kept on file for a minimum of 2 years.

5. Follow-up: Offer a meeting or written follow-up to ensure satisfaction or explain why no further action will be taken.

Pro Tip: Use a Student Complaint Form that includes date, program, issue summary, requested outcome, and signature.

C. When a Complaint Is Escalated to a Regulator (e.g., PTIB)

If your school is regulated and a student files a complaint directly with a regulatory body:

Expect:

- The regulator (e.g., PTIB) will contact you for your side of the story
- You may be asked to submit documentation (enrollment contract, attendance, correspondence, refund policies, etc.)
- A timeline will be given for resolution (often 30–60 days)
- A decision may include:
  - Upholding your actions
  - Recommending a refund
  - Imposing penalties or conditions on your school
  - Public posting of violations (in serious cases)

How to Protect Yourself:

- Ensure your policies are clearly stated and signed off on at enrollment
- Keep detailed, dated documentation of student interactions and issues
- Never promise more than what your written curriculum and policies offer

- Always document your response to complaints—even informal ones

D. *What Happens if You Don't Have a Policy?*

- You risk losing your accreditation or regulated status
- You may be required to issue a full refund, even if not warranted
- Students may post negative online reviews or file small claims lawsuits
- Your business insurance may not cover you if no formal process was followed

Final Note:

Handling complaints isn't about defending yourself—it's about showing that your school operates with professionalism, integrity, and student-centered care. A clearly written dispute policy protects both your students and your school—and ensures you're always ready if the regulator comes knocking.

Chapter 12: Scaling, Auditing & Legacy

What It Takes to Get Audited or Accredited

Getting audited or becoming an accredited institution is a milestone — one that elevates your school from a passion project to a professionally recognized educational provider. It's not just about having great content; it's about systems, transparency, and accountability.

Whether you're pursuing government accreditation or preparing for a private audit or association review, here's what you'll need to know and prepare.

What Is Accreditation?

Accreditation is a formal process where a governing body or recognized agency evaluates your school to ensure it meets a defined standard of quality, safety, and educational value.

There are two primary types:

- Government Accreditation – Usually regulated at the provincial, state, or federal level

- ## Industry or Association Accreditation –
  Issued by professional bodies within a field (e.g., massage therapy boards, holistic associations)

Why Consider Accreditation?

- It increases credibility and student trust
- It may allow students to access student loans or grants
- It makes your certificates/diplomas more transferable or recognized
- It may be required by insurance providers or licensing bodies
- In some provinces or countries, it's mandatory for certain programs (e.g., massage therapy, esthetics, medical training)

What Accreditation Bodies Look For

Here's a typical checklist of what you'll need to provide or demonstrate:

1. Registered Business Status

- Business license in your jurisdiction
- Zoning approval for educational use
- Registered school name

2. Curriculum Structure

- Learning outcomes are clearly defined
- Modules and course hours outlined
- Assessment and evaluation methods in place
- Curriculum mapped to industry or professional standards

3. Instructor Credentials

- Relevant education/training
- Teaching experience or teaching certification (in some cases)
- Resume, transcripts, and continuing education

4. Student Records & Administrative Systems

- Enrollment contracts
- Attendance tracking
- Case study documentation
- Grades, transcripts, and certificates/diplomas
- Secure digital record keeping for 55+ years (e.g., Data Witness)

5. Policies & Procedures

- Refund policies
- Dismissal and grievance processes
- Student conduct guidelines
- Appeals and complaint process

6. Facility Inspections

- Fire department and health inspections
- Accessibility and signage compliance
- Space appropriate for group learning and hands-on instruction

7. Marketing Ethics

- No misleading claims (e.g., "become certified in 2 hours!")
- Honest tuition disclosure
- Accurate instructor credentials

8. *Financial Transparency*

- Proof of financial stability
- Separation of business and student trust funds (in some regions)
- Payment tracking and receipts

How the Audit Process Works (General Overview)

1. **Application**: You submit documents and pay a review fee
2. **Initial Review**: They assess your materials and request corrections or additions
3. **On-Site Visit** (for in-person schools): Inspect space, interview staff, review live teaching
4. **Decision Issued**: You'll receive full, conditional, or denied approval
5. **Ongoing Reporting**: Annual stats, student success rates, financial audits, and renewals

Tip: Audit Yourself First

Even if you're not pursuing formal accreditation yet, do a mock audit once a year:

- Pretend you're a student and walk through your enrollment and training process
- Review your policies, forms, and contracts
- Make sure you'd be proud to hand your school records to an official reviewer

Note: Accreditation isn't for everyone — and that's okay. You can run a highly respected, successful private training school without it. But knowing what's involved helps you stay professional, scalable, and respected.

Delivery Formats: Online, Hybrid, Hobby,

In British Columbia, the 40-hour / $4,000 rule applies to all delivery formats—including online-only, hybrid, or in-class programs. If your course meets either threshold, it must be registered with PTIB regardless of how it's delivered.

Does "Online-Only" Count?

Yes—fully online courses are treated the same as in-person ones if they're career-related programs. These are classified as Class A programs, and your institution is required to register with PTIB before offering them.

What About Hybrid or Distance Delivery?

- Hybrid programs (online lectures + in-person labs/practicals) still count if they exceed the 40-hour or $4,000 limits.
- Continuous intake models (e.g., self-paced online courses) also fall under PTIB oversight if they meet the criteria.

But What If It's a Hobby or Non-Vocational?

There is one key exception: if your program is non-vocational (such as a recreational or spiritual course), you can be exempt—even if it's over 40 hours or $4,000. However, to maintain exemption, your course must:

- Avoid statements like *"become a [professional title]"*
- Not imply insurance eligibility or business use

- Focus strictly on personal growth, enrichment, or self-improvement

For instance, that Montessori Assistant course delivered online is explicitly noted as not requiring PTIB approval.

Key Takeaways

- Online = In-Person: If it's career-related and exceeds the threshold, registration is required.
- Hybrid counts too under Class A.
- Recreational/spiritual courses can be exempt, *but only* if they're intentionally marketed that way.
- Always review your marketing language to ensure compliance—and consult PTIB if unsure.

Accreditation = Voluntary Quality Seal

Accreditation through PTIB is voluntary, and it's for schools that want to go above and beyond the legal minimum.

What accreditation does:

- Signals a higher level of quality assurance
- Allows your students to apply for government student aid (StudentAid BC)
- Increases your credibility and trust with students, insurers, and employers

To get accredited, you must:

- Already be a registered institution in good standing
- Undergo a **more intensive quality review** of your curriculum, outcomes, student success tracking, financial health, and instructor credentials
- Commit to **ongoing audits and renewals**

Summary of the Difference:

Aspect	Registration	Accreditation
Required?	Yes (if 40+ hours or $4,000+)	No (optional)
Purpose	Legal operation & compliance	Quality assurance & public credibility
Reviewed by	PTIB	PTIB
StudentAid Eligible?	✖ No	✅ Yes
Level of oversight	Basic compliance	Advanced review + regular audits
Marketing impact	Legal status	High-trust signal to students

Registration vs. Accreditation

(Same Association, Different Levels)

Both registration and accreditation fall under the PTIB, but they serve very different purposes:

Registration = Legal Compliance

Registration is the minimum legal requirement that allows you to operate certain courses or programs in BC.

You must register your institution and program if you:

- Exceed the 40-hour or $4,000 threshold
- Offer vocational training meant to lead to employment
- Are not otherwise exempt (e.g., recreational or hobby courses)

Once registered, you must:

- Meet basic standards for curriculum, policies, contracts, refunds, etc.
- Undergo regular compliance inspections
- Maintain student record-keeping and reporting

Think of this as the baseline license to run a school that teaches career-related programs.

As An Example
In BC: The 40-Hour / $4,000 Rule

Under British Columbia's Private Training Act, if your course is:

- 40 hours or more in duration or
- $4,000 or more in total tuition (per student)

— then you are legally required to register your program with the Private Training Institutions Branch (PTIB).

Website: www.privatetraininginstitutions.gov.bc.ca

When You're Exempt: Understanding "Recreational," "Hobby," or "Non-Vocational" Training

PTIB's primary focus is vocational training — that is, training meant to lead to employment or self-employment. If your course doesn't meet that definition, you may be exempt, even if the course is long or expensive.

Examples of Courses That Are Typically Exempt

1. Recreational Courses

- The purpose is enjoyment or personal enrichment, not employment.
- Examples:
    - Pottery, painting, or music lessons
    - Yoga or fitness classes (with no instructor certification component)
    - Writing or journaling workshops
    - Cooking classes for home use

2. Hobby-Based Learning

- Training that is not career-focused, and unlikely to be used for paid work.
- Examples:
    - Aromatherapy for personal use
    - Astrology or tarot for self-exploration
    - Reiki Level I (if not part of a professional practice program)
    - Gardening, knitting, or DIY

3. Spiritual or Personal Development Courses

- If your course is framed around personal transformation, growth, or lifestyle enhancement, and not employment, it is often exempt.
- Examples:
    - o Meditation retreats
    - o Chakra balancing workshops
    - o Intuitive development circles

4. Professional Development for Already-Regulated Fields

- If your course is only available to people already certified/licensed (e.g., RMTs, estheticians), and it doesn't grant new titles or credentials, it may be considered continuing education and be exempt.
- Example:
    - o A workshop on new massage techniques for already-licensed massage therapists
    - o Lash lift course for certified estheticians

Gray Area: How You Market Matters

Even if your course content is "recreational," if you advertise it as a career path, you might lose your exemption.

For example:

- "Learn Reiki to deepen your personal healing journey" → likely exempt
- "Become a Certified Reiki Practitioner and start your own practice" → may require registration

Marketing language matters. If you promise career benefits, insurance eligibility, or suggest students will earn income from their training, the course may be seen as vocational.

PTIB's Exemption Guide Highlights

You are generally exempt if:

- The course is not vocational
- You do not advertise that it leads to employment or self-employment
- The course is under 40 hours and under $4,000 (regardless of content)
- You offer free training or internal training for your staff only

Best Practice

If you're unsure whether your course is exempt:

1. Review your course marketing materials — strip out employment claims unless you're registered
2. Contact PTIB directly — they can issue an exemption determination
3. Keep records of your course content, pricing, and promotional strategy — in case you're ever reviewed

Are Core Courses Included in the 40-Hour / $4,000 PTIB Threshold?

Yes — when taught separately, each core course is evaluated on its own under the Private Training Institutions Branch (PTIB) rules in British Columbia.

Here's how it works:

The PTIB regulation threshold requires that *any single course* offered to the public must be registered if it is:

- 40 hours or more in length, OR
- $4,000 or more in tuition.

This applies whether the course is part of a larger program or offered as a standalone class.

If a core course is offered individually:

It must be registered with PTIB if it exceeds either threshold (40 hours or $4,000). For example:

- A standalone Anatomy & Physiology course that runs for 45 hours or costs $4,200 would require registration.
- If you offer Business for Wellness Practitioners as a 3-day, 18-hour seminar for $995 — it's exempt.

If core courses are only available within a larger registered program:

They are not evaluated separately — they're included under the total hours and tuition of that full program.

However, if your students can take those courses individually (outside the program), then PTIB may require that you:

- Register the course independently (if it meets the thresholds),
- Or ensure it's truly exempt (under 40 hours *and* under $4,000),
- Or include a disclaimer that it is part of a hobby, personal interest, or recreational learning experience (if appropriate, and if no diploma or career preparation is implied).

Summary:

Scenario	PTIB Registration Required?
Core course taught *within* a registered program	✅ Included under the full program's registration
Core course taught *separately*, 40+ hours or $4,000+	✅ Yes — must register
Core course taught *separately*, under 40 hours and under $4,000	❌ No — exempt
Core course taught as part of a *non-vocational/hobby* workshop	❌ Possibly exempt, but proceed carefully

If all individual courses are under $4,000 and 40 hours, here's what that means under PTIB (Private Training Institutions Branch) regulations in British Columbia:

You are NOT required to register with PTIB — as long as:

1. Each individual course (certificate) offered is:
   o Less than 40 instructional hours, and
   o Costs less than $4,000, and
   o Is not part of a bundled career program that leads to employment or professional certification.

BUT — here's where it gets tricky:

Even if all your individual courses are exempt on their own, PTIB may require registration if:

You bundle the courses into a larger program that:

- Prepares students for a career (e.g., "Holistic Practitioner Diploma Program"),
- Has a total cost of $4,000 or more, or
- Has 40+ hours of instruction across the full program (even if taught in segments),
- Or results in a diploma or title that implies vocational training.

You advertise the pathway to a career:

If your marketing states that completing multiple individual certificates will result in a diploma or lead to a profession (e.g., "Earn your Spa Therapist Diploma by completing these five courses!"), PTIB may view this as a vocational program, not separate hobby courses.

To stay exempt:

If your intention is to remain unregistered, you should:

- Offer each course separately, with its own certificate and no reference to a larger program.
- Avoid implying career or job-readiness unless the total bundle is PTIB-compliant.
- Clearly state that courses are recreational, self-improvement, or personal development (if applicable).
- Avoid issuing a diploma that combines the certificates unless you're registered or exempt under a different rule.

Summary:

If ALL courses are	Do you need to register with PTIB?
< 40 hours AND < $4,000 each	✖ Not required
Part of a larger program totaling ≥ 40 hrs or $4,000	✔ Required
Advertised as vocational or diploma-level	✔ Required
Purely personal interest, no career claims	✖ Likely exempt (still double-check)

Growing into a Multi-Instructor or Franchised Model

Once your school is running smoothly, you'll reach a crossroads: Do you keep it small and personal—or scale by expanding your teaching team or replicating your model elsewhere?

Both options are valid, but each requires a strategic shift in how you operate, lead, and protect your intellectual property.

Hiring Additional Instructors

Bringing in other teachers allows you to:

- Expand your class offerings or locations
- Serve more students
- Focus on leadership or curriculum development

But it also means:

- You must codify your teaching method (see earlier: modules, learning outcomes, assessments)
- You need clear instructor agreements and training
- You become responsible for quality control and student satisfaction across all classes

What You'll Need:

- **Instructor Training Manual**: A teaching version of your course manual
- **Onboarding Process**: Set expectations for how they teach, communicate, and manage students
- **Legal Agreements**: Include intellectual property rights, compensation, and conduct policies
- **Ongoing Supervision**: Offer mentorship, reviews, or audits to ensure consistency

Tip: Choose instructors who not only know your subject—but who also align with your teaching philosophy and student experience standards.

Licensing or Certifying Others to Teach Your Program

This model allows others to license your curriculum to teach under your brand—or their own, with credit to you.

Great for:

- Expanding into new cities or regions
- Letting trusted graduates lead
- Earning passive income through licensing or royalties

You'll need:

- A teaching license agreement
- Rules around branding, use of materials, and pricing

- A certification process for instructors (so quality remains consistent)
- A licensing or franchise fee structure

Franchising Your School Model

A franchise is a business model where other people operate a replica of your school using your:

- Brand name
- Curriculum
- Teaching systems
- Business processes

Franchising involves:

- Legal franchise registration (varies by country)
- Franchise disclosure documents (FDDs)
- A higher level of legal, marketing, and systems preparation

This route:

- Offers the widest reach and brand impact
- Requires significant investment in legal, operations, and franchise support
- Can become a legacy business—but is not for the faint of heart

What to Systematize Before You Scale

Regardless of model (multi-instructor, licensed, or franchise), document:

- Your entire curriculum and instructor version of each lesson
- Your student onboarding and evaluation process
- Your school brand, voice, and values
- Your legal protections (copyright, trademarks, contracts)
- Your feedback systems (for students and instructors)

Final Thought:

Scaling doesn't mean losing intimacy—it means creating a repeatable experience that still feels personal and powerful. Your job evolves from teacher to mentor and visionary, guiding others to carry your message forward with integrity.

Selling or Licensing Your Course Materials

Once your course is proven, documented, and in demand, you have two powerful ways to expand your income and impact— selling or licensing your course content.

Each has its own structure, benefits, and legal considerations. Here's how to do it right.

1. Selling Your Course as a Digital Product

This option is great for:

- Self-paced courses with video, PDFs, and quizzes
- Coaches, authors, or practitioners with a signature framework
- One-time payments or lifetime access models

How it works:

You package your course and sell access through platforms like:

- Thinkific
- Teachable
- Kajabi
- LearnDash
- Podia
- Your own WordPress site with membership plugins

You retain full control. Students can take the course, but they cannot teach or resell it.

Key Considerations:

- Include clear Terms of Use and copyright notice.
- Secure your content with watermarks, gated access, or file protection.
- Offer completion certificates if appropriate, but not "certification" unless you're qualified to grant it.

2. Licensing Your Course to Other Instructors or Organizations

Licensing means someone else teaches your course under your brand or theirs, with your permission.

Great for:

- Expanding into new regions or industries
- Leveraging your existing student base or graduates
- Creating passive or semi-passive income

What You'll Need:

- A formal Licensing Agreement (usually drafted with a lawyer)
- Defined terms like:
  - License duration (1 year, 3 years, lifetime?)
  - Territory (Canada-only? Global?)
  - Cost structure (one-time fee, annual fee, revenue share?)
  - Use rights (can they modify your slides? Resell your worksheets?)
  - Quality controls (do they need approval or training first?)

Add-ons you may offer:

- Branded marketing materials
- Trainer onboarding
- Certification tools for their students
- Access to your LMS or private portal

Protecting Your Intellectual Property

Regardless of whether you sell or license your course:

- Register your copyrights (especially the manual and visual materials)
- Use watermarks, password-protected platforms, or digital tracking tools
- Always include copyright and license terms on your documents

Pro Tip: Make it easier for others to legally use your work than to steal it.

Why Licensing Works

Licensing allows your work to spread faster than you can teach it yourself.
When structured properly, it becomes a win-win:

- You gain income and brand recognition
- Your licensees gain a ready-to-teach, proven curriculum
- Students receive a high-quality, standardized experience

Exit Strategy for School Owners: Planning for What's Next

Starting a private training school is often fueled by passion—but at some point, every founder must think about what happens *after*. Whether you plan to retire, pivot careers, or simply sell your business, a clear exit strategy protects your students, your reputation, and your legacy.

1. Selling Your School

If your school is profitable, legally established, and has strong systems in place, it may be valuable to another educator or investor. Here's what you need to do:

- **Ensure clean financials:** Up-to-date bookkeeping, tax filings, and clear profit/loss records are essential.
- **Formalize IP ownership:** Ensure the school owns all courses, logos, systems, and materials—not individual teachers.
- **Secure staff contracts:** Having instructors under contract (ideally with non-compete clauses) makes the business more attractive.
- **Organize student records:** These must be complete, easily accessible, and legally transferable (see below).

Pro Tip: If you're incorporated, it's easier to sell your business entity as a whole. If you're a sole proprietor, you may only be able to sell the assets, not the entity.

2. Succession Planning

If you plan to keep your school in the family or pass it to a trusted team member, start preparing early:

- Mentor your replacement: Gradually hand over responsibilities to ensure continuity.
- Document processes: Everything from enrollment to refunds to grading should be written out clearly.
- Notify regulators and associations: If accredited or registered, you must inform them of leadership changes and receive approval.

Succession planning protects both your students and the school's reputation.

3. Legal Transfer of Student Records

Student data is protected under privacy laws (PIPEDA in Canada). When transferring ownership:

- Get legal advice on transferring records to the new owner
- Inform students if ownership changes—especially for regulated programs
- Ensure continued access to records (transcripts, certificates, contracts) for the required storage period (often 3–10 years)

If your school is regulated, records must be:

- Stored on Canadian servers
- Accessible to regulators upon request

- Transferred with government or association oversight

What Happens If You Die?

Preparing Your School for the Unexpected

When you own and operate a private school—especially as a sole proprietor or founder-led institution—*you* are the backbone. But what happens if something unexpected happens to you?

That's not a theoretical question.
When I owned an accredited college, a representative from PCTIA (now PTIB) sat across from me during my annual audit and asked bluntly:

"What happens if you die? Who will take over the school and teach?"

It wasn't morbid curiosity—it was a matter of student protection and legal continuity.
And it forced me to pivot quickly and prove that I had a *succession plan*, staff contracts, and documented systems in place to ensure that the school could continue even in my absence.

If you are the sole course creator, administrator, and instructor, and you pass away suddenly, your students could be left without guidance, without recourse, and without the education they paid for.

Here's how to protect your students—and your legacy:

1. Appoint a Legal Successor or Backup Administrator

- If incorporated, name a *Director or Successor Administrator* in your corporate documents.

- If sole proprietor, create a *legal will* that designates who will assume control of the school or wind it down responsibly.
- Share access to admin systems, bank accounts, and course materials with a trusted party or through a legal document.

2. Train Staff and Delegate Roles

- Have at least one other qualified instructor trained and contracted to deliver your core curriculum.
- Cross-train administrative staff (or virtual assistants) on tasks like student communications, grading, and issuing certificates.
- Keep all important processes documented—don't let your systems live only in your head.

3. Store Student Records Accessibly

- Ensure someone has secure access to:
  - Enrolled student records
  - Course completion data
  - Transcripts and issued certificates
  - Contracts and refund obligations
- Use a secure system that's password-protected and preferably cloud-based with backup.

4. Inform Accreditation or Licensing Bodies

If you are regulated or recognized by an oversight body (like PTIB or a provincial ministry), you may be *required* to:

- Provide a *contingency teaching plan* in case of incapacitation or death
- Maintain a *physical address or registrar contact* that remains valid even after your passing

5. Have a Closure Plan (Just in Case)

- Outline what happens to active students (e.g., refunds, transfers, or completion with another school).
- Ensure someone has the authority and information to:
  - Communicate with students
  - Issue outstanding documents
  - Notify licensing and financial institutions
  - Close accounts responsibly

What If the School Closes?

Planning for a Student Train-Out the Right Way

No one starts a school expecting to shut it down—but life happens. Whether due to personal health, retirement, financial struggles, or unforeseen circumstances, a school closure must be handled with care, ethics, and legal compliance—especially if students are mid-program.

The Term You Need to Know: Student Train-Out

A *Student Train-Out* is a formal plan that ensures current students can finish their education—even if the original school can no longer provide it. It's not just a courtesy; in many regulated environments, it's a legal requirement.

When I ran an accredited college, PCTIA (now PTIB in British Columbia) required me to file a Train-Out Plan in case of closure. This meant I had to prepare in advance for how enrolled students would:

- Complete their courses
- Receive valid certificates or transcripts
- Get access to any promised materials or training

Key Elements of a Proper Train-Out Plan:

1. Contract with a Successor School or Instructor

You must create a legally binding agreement with:

- Another school of equal or greater standing, or
- A qualified instructor with the ability and credentials to teach your curriculum

This agreement must clearly state:

- How and when the students will complete their training
- Any financial arrangements between the institutions (NOT between the student and the new school)
- That the certificate will still reflect the original school name (unless otherwise arranged)

2. Do Not Close the Business Bank Account Immediately

It's crucial that the school's bank account remains open during the student train-out period. This ensures:

- Refunds can be issued if needed
- Funds can be paid to the successor school/instructor for completion training
- The school meets legal obligations tied to tuition held "in trust until earned"

Closing the account prematurely can:

- Violate trust or consumer protection laws
- Result in student complaints or lawsuits
- Jeopardize your licensing or professional reputation

3. Do Not Transfer Student Files Across Borders

Even if you move or the school is sold, student records must remain in the originating province or country, especially:

- Contracts
- Attendance records
- Transcripts and certificates
- Financial records

Why?

- Many provincial laws (and some federal privacy regulations) prohibit the storage of educational records outside Canada.
- Accreditation or oversight bodies (e.g., PTIB, provincial ministries) require access to original records for a period (often 5–10 years) post-closure.

Use secure, cloud-based Canadian servers if possible—or partner with a registrar who can legally store and access them on behalf of the school.

4. Notify All Required Parties

When planning to close, be sure to:

- Notify the regulatory body (PTIB, provincial education department, etc.) and submit your train-out plan
- Inform students in writing with timelines and options
- Notify insurance providers, municipal business licensing offices, and tax authorities

5. Protect Your Legacy and Your Students

A graceful closure is a powerful final act of integrity. By ensuring your students are cared for—educationally and financially—you:

- Maintain your professional reputation
- Avoid legal action
- Leave the door open for future projects, consulting, or publishing

Final Note: If you're a school founder—even of a small training academy or online course—you are responsible for your students' outcomes. A student train-out isn't just paperwork. It's a *promise* to uphold the integrity of your teaching, right to the very end.

Reactivation or Dormancy Rules for Closed or Paused Schools

Whether due to personal health, financial strain, or simply needing a break, some school owners choose to temporarily pause operations. Others close down entirely—only to later decide to reopen. But what happens legally when a school goes dormant, and what's required to bring it back to life?

1. What Happens If You Pause Your School?

If you're planning to pause or temporarily suspend your operations:

- Unregulated schools (e.g., workshops, <40 hr courses) may be able to quietly go dormant with no reporting obligations—especially sole proprietorships.

- Regulated or accredited schools, however, must notify the regulator (e.g., PTIB in BC) in writing and may need to submit:
    - A formal cessation of instruction notice
    - Student Train-Out plans for active learners
    - Ongoing access to records and transcripts

Student records must still be accessible for a minimum duration (typically 5–7 years), even if your school is no longer operating.

2. Reactivation Fees and Compliance Expectations

To reactivate a school, you may be required to:

- Pay a reactivation or reinstatement fee to the regulator or Ministry
- Update curriculum and teacher credentials to meet current standards
- Undergo a new site inspection or submit updated financials
- Provide proof that:
    - Student files are intact and secure
    - Refund policies, insurance, and contracts are compliant

Reactivation may be treated like a new application— especially if dormant for more than a year or two.

3. How Long Can You Stay Dormant?

This varies depending on your province, regulatory status, and structure (e.g., sole prop vs. incorporated):

- **PTIB (British Columbia):** Typically allows up to **12 months** of inactivity before you must reapply as a new institution
- **Federal/CRA (Canada Revenue Agency):** If your corporation hasn't filed taxes for **two years**, it may be automatically dissolved
- **Corporations Canada:** Dormant federally registered businesses may be flagged for dissolution if inactive

Being dormant **does not remove legal obligations.** You must still maintain:

- Recordkeeping
- CRA filings (even if $0)
- Student record storage
- Compliance with PIPEDA (privacy)

Summary:

- If you plan to **pause** your school:
  Notify your regulatory body (if accredited)
  Maintain student access to records
  Keep your business license, bank accounts, and filings current
  Document your intent to return—and when
- If you **closed** your school but want to **reactivate it:**
  Expect a partial or full reapplication
  Budget for possible inspections, updates, and fees
  Be aware that your former accreditation may not carry over automatically

Leaving a Legacy

You didn't build your school just to walk away—you built it to make a difference. Whether you sell, step down, or pass it on:

- Leave your systems strong
- Leave your name in good standing
- Leave your students empowered

Because a true educator's impact continues long after the final lesson.

Final Thought: Legacy isn't just about how many students you teach—it's also about *what happens after you're gone.*

Having a succession or emergency plan isn't about being pessimistic. It's about being professional. Your school—and the people who trust it—deserve nothing less.

Chapter 13: How to Avoid Failure and Bankruptcy

Lessons Learned the Hard Way—So You Don't Have To

The Biggest Mistakes New School Owners Make

Avoid These Common Pitfalls That Derail Even the Most Passionate Teachers

Starting a school—whether online, hybrid, or in-person—is an exciting leap. You're not just sharing knowledge; you're stepping into a whole new identity as a business owner and educational leader. But passion alone isn't enough to sustain a school. These are the mistakes that can quietly (or catastrophically) sabotage your dream if you're not aware:

1. Overspending Before Validating the Idea

You've got a vision. So you rent a space, buy equipment, design a logo, print brochures… all before anyone has actually signed up. Reality check: The only thing that validates a course is someone *paying* for it.

Better strategy:

- Start with a pilot program or beta course
- Use minimal tools (Zoom, Canva, free LMS)
- Focus on building a waitlist or interest list before investing in physical assets

Think lean. Every dollar you save now is fuel for longevity later.

2. Offering Too Many Courses Too Soon

You want to help everyone—so you try to build a full curriculum right away. This creates overwhelm for you and confusion for potential students.

Result: You stretch yourself thin, can't market effectively, and end up with half-built programs no one buys.

Instead:

- Start with one core signature course
- Perfect it, deliver results, collect testimonials
- Expand only after that first offering is profitable and streamlined

One transformational course beats five incomplete ones.

3. Failing to Track Cash Flow and Expenses

Many new school owners don't treat their business like a business. They don't separate personal and business expenses, don't budget for marketing, or don't plan for slower months.

Common traps:

- Not knowing what your monthly expenses actually are
- Spending tuition money before the course finishes
- Forgetting taxes, insurance, software subscriptions

Solution:

- Open a dedicated business bank account
- Use simple software (like Wave, QuickBooks, or a spreadsheet)
- Know your **monthly breakeven number** and your **profit per student**

If you don't measure it, you can't manage it.

4. Assuming "If You Build It, They Will Come"

This is the big one. Many passionate instructors believe that having a beautiful course or a great skillset is enough.

It's not.

No one will know you exist unless you learn to market, share your story, and reach out consistently.

Marketing isn't sleazy—it's service. If you believe in your course, then your job is to help the right people find it.

Don't hide behind perfectionism. Start before you're ready.

Bottom line?

The difference between a teacher and a successful school owner isn't passion—it's planning.

Avoid these early traps, and your dream becomes sustainable. Ignore them, and your school might never make it past the first year.

Cross-Provincial Compliance & Legal Risks

What You Don't Know Can Get You Fined—or Shut Down

Running a private school, training center, or college is not like running a regular business. Every province and territory in Canada has specific laws that govern educational institutions, and if you step outside those rules—even accidentally—you could face fines, lawsuits, and permanent blacklisting.

Here's what you need to know before you grow.

You Can Teach Students Across Provinces—But There Are Conditions

In Canada, education is governed provincially, which means each province or territory sets its own rules for private training institutions. However, you are not automatically barred from teaching students in other provinces—especially when it comes to non-accredited, non-vocational education or online courses.

Here's the correct breakdown:

When You Can Teach Across Provinces (Without Registering in Each One)

You are generally not required to register in another province if:

- Your course is under that province's regulatory threshold (e.g., less than 40 hours or under $4000 in BC)
- Your course is non-vocational (e.g., hobby, wellness, self-improvement)
- You are offering online programs that do not promise job placement or certification in a regulated profession
- You clearly state your program is not a government-accredited diploma or certificate

Example: A Reiki Master teaching online to students in Ontario, Alberta, and Nova Scotia does not need to register in each province, as long as the program:

- Doesn't exceed that province's thresholds
- Doesn't imply licensure or professional designation
- Doesn't market itself as a career college

When You Might Need to Register or Seek Exemption

You may need to register with a province's education regulator if:

- Your program exceeds the hour/tuition threshold (e.g., 40+ hours or $4000+ in BC)
- You offer career training that leads to a specific job title (e.g., Esthetician, Massage Therapist)
- You advertise that your program leads to employment, certification, or professional designation
- You deliver in-person classes within that province (not just online)

Example: If you run a full esthetics diploma program in BC, and start accepting Alberta students online, Alberta's Ministry may require you to notify or register—especially if you're issuing professional certificates.

The Key Is: Know Your Course Category and Your Claims

If you're teaching personal development, wellness, or spiritual topics, you're typically exempt—unless you step into regulated career training. But if you're teaching in a professionally governed space (like aesthetics, bodywork, PMU, or natural health), tread carefully.

Moving or Sharing Student Files Without Permission Is Illegal

In every province, accredited or regulated schools must maintain secure student files for a minimum number of years—up to 55 years in BC.

You cannot:

- Transfer student files to another location without notifying the regulatory body
- Take student files with you to another province
- Store student records in your house if your license requires a separate location

Student files must include:

- Legal name and contact info
- Copy of registration
- Signed contracts and consent forms
- Transcripts, certificates/diplomas
- Refund/payment history

Files must be:

- Secure (locked filing cabinet or encrypted database)
- Accessible for inspection during audits
- Retained for decades—even after a student graduates or drops out

Digital solutions like Data Witness, DocuSign Vault, or government-approved third-party archives can store these legally.

No School Bank Account = Non-Compliance

If you are offering education over 40 hours or charging over $4000 in BC (or its equivalent in another province), you are expected to:

- Open a separate business bank account
- Track all tuition payments and refunds
- Provide access to your books during annual audits
- NEVER co-mingle personal and school funds

Shutting down your account or transferring funds

without proper closure procedures could result in:

- Audit failure
- Loss of licensing
- Legal action for financial mismanagement

Changing School Location Without Approval

You cannot move your school—*even down the street*—without getting written approval from your province's regulatory body. They will want to:

- Inspect the new location
- Approve zoning
- Verify accessibility and emergency protocols
- Ensure student files and signage are updated

Moving without notifying them can result in your license being revoked.

Annual Reports, Audits, and Re-Approvals

In regulated provinces, you must submit annual reports on:

- Enrollment numbers
- Graduate employment rates
- Refunds and withdrawals
- Program updates
- Financial statements (often reviewed or audited by a CPA)

You may also undergo:

- Random audits
- Site inspections
- Curriculum reviews

If you fail to comply or miss deadlines, your approval can be suspended or terminated, and your students may lose eligibility for insurance, loans, or employment recognition.

Bottom Line

Running a school isn't just teaching—it's regulated education.

If you don't understand your provincial laws—or try to "bend" the rules—you risk:

- Fines and lawsuits
- Blacklisting from government registries
- Refunding full tuition to all students
- Damaging your reputation beyond repair

Start smart. Grow ethically. And always know the rules before you expand.

My Cautionary Tale: When Passion Meets Paperwork

I had owned and operated my school in Kelowna, BC for fourteen years—many of those as an accredited college. It was steady: not growing in the final five years, but maintaining a consistent intake of students and stable income. Like many entrepreneurs, I wanted more. I decided to expand.

An opportunity came to open inside an existing college in Delta, BC. It seemed like the perfect way to grow—until I went to get a business licence. The city told me "No." The current school had been *grandfathered* into that location. They couldn't sell or sublease it to anyone else. I was stunned. But still determined.

So, We (had a potential business partner) searched for another space. We found one, signed a lease, and put down a $10,000 deposit. Zoning was approved for education use. But when we applied for the business licence, the city informed us that the building would require seismic upgrades—at a cost of $100,000's and extensive delays. We couldn't afford that. We lost the deposit.

Finally, I found what seemed like the ideal space. I signed the lease (no business partner), completed renovations, and opened for business.

But here's what I didn't know:

The front door of the building remained locked at all times, and there was no buzzer system. No students could get in without calling me to be let in. After everything I had invested, I was effectively running a school *no one could access.*

My first class? One student. From Ontario. That was it.

I couldn't sustain operations in both Kelowna and Vancouver with just one student in the new location. Then, just days later, the landlord emailed me saying the lease paperwork had a mistake and needed to be re-signed. I saw it as divine intervention—a way out.

That night, I packed everything up, emailed the landlord a note, mailed him the keys, and walked away.

I also made the tough call to shut down the Kelowna location.

I was still actively doing legal train-outs for my distant education students, ensuring they finished their programs properly.

But a few months later, during the process of buying a new home, my lawyer asked, "Whatever happened with that school lease?" He'd just received legal notice: the landlord was suing me.

It turns out, the landlord's lawyer had also contacted PCTIA (now PTIB). Suddenly, the regulatory body was involved. I had already moved to back to Kelowna by then—and since I hadn't updated my lawyer with my new address or phone number, I had no idea legal proceedings were moving forward.

As if that wasn't enough, my husband's work slowed, and we moved again—to Edmonton, Alberta. I took the 21 student files with me so I could continue the train-outs. Since the school had no income, I closed the school's business bank account and began paying PTIB's monthly fees from my personal account.

Mistake. Big mistake.

PCTIA placed a lien on our joint bank account—meaning neither of us could access any of our money. Then they placed a lien on the house we were selling. Because my husband was a listed director of the school, he was now legally involved too.

The legal and financial weight became unbearable. With no other option, we both filed for bankruptcy in Alberta.

But the surprises weren't over. Even though our adult son was still living in our house in BC, we lost the funds from the home sale—because we weren't physically living there at the time.

In the end, we paid more to the bankruptcy trustee over two years than we ever owed the people who were suing us.

The Moral?

If you plan to run a private school, don't skip the legal and financial details.

✓ Always update addresses.
✓ Never shut down your business account too early.
✓ Don't pay institutional obligations from personal funds.
✓ Know your zoning, licensing, and lease terms *before* you sign.
✓ And don't assume moving your school—or your student files—to another province is allowed without approval.

What started as a dream to help more students became the most painful financial chapter of our lives.

But through it all, I learned what *not* to do—and now, I'm sharing it with you so you never have to go through the same.

Final Thoughts: Your Legacy Begins Now

You've made it to the end of this book—and what a journey it's been.

Maybe your head is spinning a little. Maybe you're already scribbling course ideas in the margins. Maybe you're thinking, *"Can I really do this?"*

The answer is yes.

Yes, you can build a school.
Yes, you can teach others in a meaningful, ethical, and legal way.
Yes, you can create a legacy that ripples far beyond the classroom.

But take a breath. Because even though we've covered everything from zoning bylaws to refund policies, remember this:

You don't have to do it all at once.

Start small.
Teach one workshop.
Build one course.
Serve one student well.

Every successful school you've ever admired started with one person, one idea, one brave decision. The difference between staying a dreamer and becoming a founder is simply this: *taking the next step.*

Will you make mistakes? Absolutely.
Will there be paperwork? Of course.
But will it be worth it? Without a doubt.

Because what you're really doing is creating a place where others can grow, transform, and awaken. You're becoming the guide you once needed. The teacher who changes lives—not just by what you say, but by who you are.

Let this book be your resource, not your ruler. Come back to it when questions arise. Use the tools, checklists, and warnings not as pressure—but as permission. Permission to build something real. Something right. Something *you*.

And when it gets hard, remember this:

You don't need to have it all figured out.
You just need to keep moving forward.

Because the world doesn't just need more teachers—it needs more torchbearers.

And if you've made it this far, it means the flame is already in your hands.

To your legacy,

Dr. Constance Santego
Founder, Educator, Visionary

P.S. My own journey didn't end in a courtroom—or even a classroom. I went on to earn my Massage Therapy Diploma, as well as a Ph.D. and Doctorate in Natural Medicine. I've since become a bestselling author of over 40 titles—each one created to pass on what I've learned, so others like you don't have to start from scratch.

So now it's your turn.
To rise.
To teach.
To build something lasting.

And remember:

One step at a time is still forward.

You've got this.

"An *Academypreneur* doesn't just teach a subject—they craft a legacy, one student, one lesson, one breakthrough at a time."

Appendix

Regulated Courses/Programs

CANADA

British Columbia

Regulated Professions in BC (with associated courses/training)

In BC, regulated professions are governed by legislation and professional colleges or associations. If you're teaching a course in these areas, you must follow specific rules, including curriculum standards, licensing, and potentially Ministry approval.

Health & Wellness Professions (Regulated)

These require registration with a regulatory college under the Health Professions Act or other provincial acts:

- Registered Massage Therapist (RMT) – 2,200-hour diploma, must graduate from an approved college and pass CMTBC exams
- Chiropractor
- Physiotherapist

- Naturopathic Doctor
- Acupuncturist / Traditional Chinese Medicine (TCM) Practitioner
- Occupational Therapist
- Registered Nurse (RN)
- Licensed Practical Nurse (LPN)
- Dental Hygienist / Dental Assistant
- Speech-Language Pathologist
- Psychologist
- Midwife
- Pharmacist
- Medical Laboratory Technologist
- Optician / Optometrist
- Dietitian

Beauty & Personal Services (Partially Regulated or Industry-Specific)

These are not provincially regulated under law, but certain training standards are expected, especially for licensing and insurance:

- Esthetics – Not regulated, but standards set by industry and insurance providers (some schools follow 600+ hour guidelines)
- Hairdressing / Barbering – Trades-certified under Industry Training Authority (ITA BC); Red Seal available
- Permanent Makeup (PMU) – Not provincially regulated, but public health bylaws apply

- Tattooing – Regulated by local health authorities, not by a provincial college

Trades & Apprenticeships (Regulated through ITA BC)

These professions are regulated and require certification:

- Electrician
- Plumber
- Heavy Duty Mechanic
- Welding
- Carpentry
- Automotive Service Technician
- Cook (Red Seal Chef)

Programs must be approved by ITA BC (Industry Training Authority) to count toward certification.

Education & Childcare (Regulated)

- Early Childhood Educator (ECE) – Must complete an approved ECE program and register with the ECE Registry
- K–12 School Teacher – Must have a B.Ed. and be certified through the BC Ministry of Education's Teacher Regulation Branch

Legal, Financial, and Government Professions

- Lawyer – Must complete law school + Law Society of BC certification
- Notary Public
- CPA (Chartered Professional Accountant)
- Real Estate Agent – Must complete UBC Sauder School of Business licensing program
- Insurance Broker – LLQP certification required

Not Regulated (but often taught professionally):

These are *not* regulated by the province, but often have industry best practices or are covered under local bylaws and insurance standards:

- Reiki
- Reflexology
- Aromatherapy
- Coaching / NLP / Hypnotherapy
- Sound healing
- Energy medicine
- Herbalism
- Makeup artistry
- Spiritual training
- Life coaching
- Meditation teacher training

Alberta

Health & Allied Health Professions (Under Health Professions Act)

These professions require training from an approved program and registration with a regulatory college:

- **Physician / Surgeon** – College of Physicians and Surgeons of Alberta
- **Registered Nurse (RN) / LPN / Psychiatric Nurse** – College/Association of Registered Nurses
- **Dentist / Dental Hygienist / Dental Assistant** – Alberta Dental Association & College
- **Pharmacist** – College of Alberta College of Pharmacists
- **Occupational Therapist, Physiotherapist, Speech-Language Pathologist, Psychologist, Social Worker, Midwife** – respective colleges under HPA

Trades & Apprenticeships (Through Apprenticeship and Industry Training)

These skilled trades require certified training programs to complete apprenticeships:

- **Electrician, Plumber, Carpenter, Welder, Mechanic, Cook,** and many more—regulated by Alberta's Apprenticeship system

Legal & Finance Professions

- Lawyer – must complete law school, pass bar, and be a member of the Law Society of Alberta
- CPA / Chartered Accountant – certification through provincial body
- Real Estate Agent / Broker – via Real Estate Council of Alberta

Other Regulated Occupations

Under the Fair Registration Practices Act, professionals must register with governing bodies to use protected titles:

- Professional Engineer (P.Eng) – APEGA
- Architect, Agrologist, Appraisers, Surveyors, etc.
- Dental Technologist, Optician, Medical Lab Technologist, Chiropractor, Acupuncturist, Pharmacist, etc.

Education & Childcare

- Early Childhood Educator (ECE) – must graduate from approved ECE programs and register with ECE Registry
- K–12 Teacher – requires a Bachelor of Education and certification by the Teacher Regulation Branch

Summary at a Glance

Profession Category	Requires Regulated Training & Licensing?
Medical & Allied Health	✓ Yes, through professional colleges
Trades & Apprenticeships	✓ Yes, through provincial apprenticeship
Legal/Financial	✓ Yes, must pass official cert/licensure
Engineering/Architecture	✓ Yes, regulated titles (P.Eng, Architect)
Education/Childcare	✓ Yes for preschool & K–12 teachers
Nonregulated Wellness	✗ No (e.g. Reiki, life coaching)

Saskatchewan

Regulated Professions & Trades in Saskatchewan

Professionals must complete approved educational pathways, be licensed, and be registered with regulatory bodies before legally working or using protected titles.

Compulsory Apprenticeship Trades

Under the Saskatchewan Apprenticeship and Trade Certification Commission (SATCC), these five trades require apprenticeship and certification to practice legally:

- Electrician
- Plumber
- Sprinkler Fitter
- Refrigeration (HVAC) Mechanic
- Sheet Metal Worker

Additionally, the Hairstylist trade is also regulated and requires certification from SATCC.

These trades often participate in the Red Seal Program for national standardization.

Health & Allied Health Professions

These roles are regulated by professional colleges under provincial legislation. Notable regulated professions include:

- Physician & Surgeon – College of Physicians and Surgeons of Saskatchewan
- Physical Therapist – Saskatchewan College of Physical Therapists

- Other health professionals (typically regulated but not listed in search results):
  - Chiropractor, Dentist, Dental Hygienist, Optometrist, Pharmacist, Nurse (RN/LPN), Psychologist, Social Worker, Midwife, Audiologist, Speech-Language Pathologist, etc.

Legal, Financial & Professional Professions

These roles are regulated by provincial bodies:

- Lawyers – Law Society of Saskatchewan
- Professional Engineers & Geoscientists – APEGS
- Registered Professional Planners (RPP) – under The Community Planning Profession Act
- Accountants (CPA), Architects, Veterinarians, Professional Planners, among others (refer to Regulatory Bodies List)

Education & Childcare

- Early Childhood Educator (ECE) – Certification required
- K–12 Teachers – Must complete a Bachelor of Education and receive a provincial teaching certificate

Other Licensed Roles

Certain fields require licensing or registration, even if not traditional professions:

- **Building Officials, Crane/Hoist Operators** – under provincial regulations
- **Private Investigators** and **Security Guards** – require licensing
- **Tattoo and Piercing Artists** – regulated via public health bylaws, not provincial colleges

6. Unregulated—but Practically Guided—Fields

The following are *not provincially regulated*, but professional standards or insurance requirements often apply:

- Reiki, Reflexology, Aromatherapy, Coaching, NLP, Massage Therapy (future regulation?), Sound Healing, Makeup Artistry, Life & Spiritual Coaching

Manitoba

Regulated Professions & Trades in Manitoba

Manitoba regulates careers to protect public safety. Many titles and services require specific training, certification, and membership in regulatory bodies. Here's an organized breakdown:

Self-Regulated Professions (Title & Practice Restricted)

Under Manitoba's *Fair Registration Practices in Regulated Professions Act*, these professionals must be licensed to legally use their titles and perform their work :

- **Health & Allied Health:** Physician/surgeon, dentist, dental hygienist/assistant, chiropractor, optometrist, pharmacist, physiotherapist, occupational therapist, speech-language pathologist, audiologist, registered nurse (RN/LPN), psychiatric nurse, midwife, paramedic, dietitian, medical lab technologist, respiratory therapist.

- **Counseling & Social Services:** Psychologist, social worker, speech-language pathologist (also in health), audiologist.

- **Technical & Professional Services:** Accountant (CPA), architect, agrologist, engineer/geoscientist, veterinarian, professional planner, funeral director/embalmer, home economist.

- **Other:** Public health inspector, private investigator, security guard, pesticide/petroleum technicians, water/wastewater operator, arborist, hunting guide, stretcher attendant, etc.

Here's a well-organized summary of **regulated professions and trades in Manitoba,** which you can include in your book or reference for course planning:

Regulated Professions & Trades in Manitoba

These are professions where you must meet provincial standards, complete approved education or training, and register with a governing body before legally working or using a protected title.

Health & Allied Health Professions (Regulated under various Acts)

To legally practice or use titles like "Registered" or "Licensed," individuals must be certified through a regulatory college:

- Physician / Surgeon
- Nurse (RN, LPN, RPN)
- Paramedic
- Pharmacist
- Chiropractor
- Dentist / Dental Hygienist / Dental Assistant
- Midwife
- Dietitian
- Physiotherapist / Occupational Therapist
- Speech-Language Pathologist / Audiologist
- Medical Laboratory Technologist
- Respiratory Therapist
- Optometrist / Ophthalmic Assistant
- Psychologist
- Social Worker

Regulated Trades (Apprenticeship Manitoba)

These trades require registration as an apprentice, completion of a provincially approved program, and Red Seal or Certificate of Qualification to work legally:

- Electrician (Construction/Industrial)
- Plumber / Pipefitter / Gasfitter
- Welder / Boilermaker
- Carpenter / Cabinetmaker
- Auto Technician / Heavy Duty Mechanic
- Cook / Baker
- Hairstylist (includes Esthetics in some cases)

Apprenticeship Manitoba oversees these and more. Red Seal endorsements apply to many.

Legal, Financial, and Technical Professions

- Lawyer – Law Society of Manitoba
- Notary Public / Commissioner for Oaths
- Chartered Professional Accountant (CPA)
- Engineer / Geoscientist – Engineers Geoscientists Manitoba
- Architect / Professional Planner
- Veterinarian / Veterinary Technician
- Funeral Director / Embalmer
- Agrologist / Home Economist

Education & Childcare

- Early Childhood Educator (ECE) – Requires provincial certification
- K–12 School Teacher – Bachelor of Education + Manitoba Teaching Certificate

Other Licensed or Permitted Roles

These may not be professions in the traditional sense, but still require licensing or certification:

- Private Investigator / Security Guard
- Water & Wastewater Technician
- Petroleum/Pesticide Applicator
- Hunting Guide / Fishing Operator
- Arborist (in urban forestry contexts)
- Tattoo / Body Piercing Artist – Regulated by public health bylaws (not a professional college)

Not Provincially Regulated (But May Require Insurance Standards)

These professions are not legally regulated in Manitoba but may be expected to meet industry best practices or standards for liability insurance:

- Reiki
- Reflexology
- Aromatherapy
- Coaching
- Crystal or energy healing
- Sound therapy
- Makeup artistry
- Holistic nutritionist (unless calling themselves "dietitian")
- Life/spiritual coaching

Summary for Course Creators:

Category	Regulated in Manitoba?
Massage Therapy	✅ Yes (Voluntary association, not college-regulated yet)
Esthetics (basic)	✖ No (health-inspected, not regulated)
Reiki / Energy Healing	✖ No
Coaching / NLP / Hypnosis	✖ No
Tattoo / Piercing	⚠ Yes (by health authorities)
Hairstyling / Barbering	✅ Yes (Apprenticeship trade)
ECE / K–12 Teacher	✅ Yes
Allopathic / Allied Health	✅ Yes
Personal Training	✖ No (private certification accepted)

Ontario

Health & Allied Health Professions

Ontario regulates 27 **health professions** under the *Regulated Health Professions Act*. Most require completion of an accredited program and membership in a professional college to practice or use protected titles:

- Physician / Surgeon
- Registered Nurse (RN) / Registered Practical Nurse (RPN)
- Dentist / Dental Hygienist / Dental Technologist / Denturist
- Pharmacist / Pharmacy Technician
- Chiropractor
- Physiotherapist
- Occupational Therapist
- Speech-Language Pathologist / Audiologist
- Dietitian
- Medical Laboratory Technologist
- Optometrist / Optician
- Medical Radiation Technologist
- Midwife
- Paramedic
- Chiropodist / Podiatrist
- Psychologist / Psychotherapist
- Traditional Chinese Medicine Practitioner & Acupuncturist
- Kinesiologist

Skilled Trades

Oversight by Skilled Trades Ontario, which manages compulsory trades, apprenticeships, and certification, including many Red Seal trades:

Compulsory trades (must be a registered apprentice or journeyperson):

- Electrician (Construction, Domestic, Industrial)
- Plumber
- Hairstylist
- Refrigeration & A/C Mechanic
- Sheet Metal Worker
- Motor Vehicle Mechanic, Autobody Repairer, Transmission Technician
- Crane and Hoisting Operators
- Motorcycle Technician
  ...and many others

Non-compulsory trades have voluntary certification options.

Legal, Technical & Financial Professions

Require university credentials and licensure through provincial bodies:

- Lawyer / Paralegal
- Accountant (CPA)
- Professional Engineer (P.Eng.) / Geoscientist (P.Geo.)
- Architect / Professional Planner
- Notary Public
- Real Estate Agent
- Insurance Broker

Education & Childcare

- K–12 Teachers – Bachelor of Education + Ontario College of Teachers certification
- Early Childhood Educators (ECEs) – Ontario-regulated certification for daycare and preschool teaching

Non-Regulated but Industry-Standards-Based

These fields don't require government accreditation, but professionals often get certified by private bodies for credibility or insurance:

- Reiki, Reflexology, Aromatherapy
- Coaching, NLP, Hypnotherapy
- Sound/Sound healing, Makeup artistry
- Life/spiritual coaching
- Massage therapy (note: regulated provincially later)

Summary Table

Category	Regulated in Ontario?	Requires Certified Program?
Medical / Allied Health	☑ Yes	Yes (for protected titles)
Skilled Trades (compulsory)	☑ Yes	Yes (apprenticeship)
Legal / Engineering / Finance	☑ Yes	Yes
K–12 / ECE Teachers	☑ Yes	Yes
Complementary / Wellness Fields	⊘ No	Optional for insurance/credibility

Quebec

CA Regulated Professions & Trades in Québec

Regulated Trades (via Commission de la construction du Québec – CCQ)

Québec regulates certain construction trades, requiring apprenticeship, skill verification, and a competency certificate from the Commission de la construction du Québec (CCQ). These include (but aren't limited to):

- Electrician • Carpenter • Crane Operator • Plumber • Sheet Metal Worker
- Welder • Heavy Equipment Mechanic • Fire-Protection Mechanic • Elevator Mechanic
  …and several others defined under Act R-20.

Regulated Professions (via Professional Orders)

Québec enshrines over 46 professional orders covering 54 professions, under the Professional Code. These include:

- Health & Wellness Jobs: Acupuncturists, Chiropractors, Dentists & Technicians, Optometrists, Midwives, Nurses, Pharmacists, Physiotherapists, Psychologists, Speech-Language Pathologists, Audiologists, Social Workers, etc.
- Legal, Technical & Administrative Roles: Lawyers (Barreau), Architects, Engineers, Agrologists, Land Surveyors, Chartered Administrators/Management Consultants, Financial Planners, Notaries, CPAs, Urban Planners, etc. .

These professionals must pass accredited training/programs and register with their respective order to legally use protected titles.

What This Means for Course Creators in Québec

Category	Implications for Your School
CCQ-regulated trades	Requires apprenticeship-aligned programs, competency certs
Professional Order professions	Must align with accredited curriculum, approval, and Order rules
Unregulated wellness/creative fields	Full curriculum flexibility with attention to clarity and professional standards

New Brunswick

Regulated Professions & Trades in New Brunswick

Licensed Professions

These roles require certification from a provincial regulatory body to legally practice or use the title:

- **Health & Allied Health**: Physician, RN/LPN, Paramedic, Pharmacist, Chiropractor, Dentist, Dental Hygienist/Assistant, Optometrist, Physiotherapist, Occupational Therapist, Speech-Language Pathologist/Audiologist, Midwife, Respiratory Therapist, Dietitian, Medical Laboratory Technologist, Medical Radiation Technologist, Cardiology Technologist
- **Counseling/Mental Health**: Psychologist, Social Worker, Counselling Therapist
- **Others**: Engineer/Geoscientist, Agrologist, Architect, Land Surveyor, Funeral Director/Embalmer, Veterinarian, Optician, Home Economist

Education & Childcare

- **Early Childhood Educator (ECE)** — Provincial certification required
- **Teacher (K–12)** — Regulated by the Department of Education and Early Childhood Development

Legal & Financial Professions

- Lawyer, Notary, Real Estate Agent, Mortgage Broker, Chartered Professional Accountant (CPA)

Skilled Trades (Apprenticeship NB)

New Brunswick oversees 82 designated trades, including 12 compulsory ones. Apprenticeship involves ~80% on-the-job training and ~20% in-school learning, leading to certification and, for many, a Red Seal endorsement:

Examples of Compulsory (Red Seal) Trades:

- Electrician
- Plumber
- Heavy-Duty Mechanic
- Carpenter
- Welder
- Automotive Service Technician
- Cook
  …and more

Other Certified Occupations

Require membership in a provincial regulator:

- Barber
- Cosmetologist
- Building Official
- Translator/Interpreter
  …among others

Unregulated Fields (But Insurance-Standard-Based)

These are not provincially regulated but may have industry guidelines or insurance expectations:

- Massage Therapy (via massage therapy association)
- Reiki, Reflexology, Coaching, Aromatherapy, Energy Healing, Makeup Artistry, Sound Healing

Quick-reference Table for New Brunswick

Category	Regulated?	Requires Certification?
Health/allied health professions	☑ Yes	Yes
K–12 Teachers & ECE	☑ Yes	Yes
Skilled Trades (Red Seal)	☑ Yes	Yes
Legal, Finance, Technical	☑ Yes	Yes
Personal Care/Grooming	☑ Yes	Yes
Massage Therapy	⚠ Association-based	Yes (provincial association)
Wellness & Creative Arts	✖ No	No

Nova Scotia

Regulated Trades & Professions in Nova Scotia

Apprenticeship Trades (via NS Apprenticeship Agency)

- Over 70 designated trades, including 54 Red Seal trades.
- 13 compulsory certified trades require certification or apprentice status to work legally:
  - Autobody Technician
  - Automotive Service Technician (incl. Service Centre)
  - Boilermaker
  - Bricklayer
  - Construction Electrician
  - Oil Heat System Technician
  - Plumber
  - Refrigeration & A/C Mechanic
  - Sheet Metal Worker
  - Sprinkler Fitter
  - Steamfitter/Pipefitter
  - Truck & Transport Mechanic.
- Completing an approved apprenticeship grants eligibility to write the provincial or Red Seal exam

Other Regulated Occupations (via various provincial authorities)

- Trades requiring special licensing or permits, including:
  - Pesticide Applicator
  - Petroleum Storage Installer
  - On-site Sewage Disposal Specialist
  - Water/Wastewater Operator
  - Well Digger & Driller
  - Hearing Aid Salesperson

- o   Mortgage Broker
- o   Timber Scaler
- o   Hunting & Fishing Guide.

Education & Childcare

- **K–12 Teachers** – provincially certified through the Teacher Certification Office.
- **Early Childhood Educators (ECEs)** – also certified via the Ministry of Education & Early Childhood Development.

Technical & Professional Technicians

- **Engineering Technicians & Technologists** – certified through TechNova, with designations like C.Tech or A.Sc.T. under provincial law.

Unregulated but Insurance-Relevant Fields

- Reiki, reflexology, aromatherapy, coaching, sound healing, massage therapy, makeup artistry, life/spiritual coaching, etc.
  While unregulated provincially, these fields often require industry-standard training and insurance compliance.

Prince Edward Island

Regulated Professions & Trades in Prince Edward Island

Regulated Professions

These careers are protected by law and require individuals to be registered with a provincial regulatory authority and hold a licence or certificate to work legally.

- **Health & Allied Health**: Dentist, Dental Hygienist, Dental Assistant, Chiropractor, Dietitian, Medical Laboratory Technologist, Medical Radiation Technologist, Respiratory Therapist, Occupational Therapist, Optician, Optometrist, Licensed Practical Nurse (LPN), Emergency Medical Technician (Paramedic), Nurse Practitioner.
- **Early Childhood Educator (ECE)**
- **Engineers** (Engineers PEI)
- **Agrologist**
- **Architect**
- **Lawyer**
- **Accountant (CPA)**
- **Elevator/Lift Installer**
- **Gas Dispenser Operator**
- **Home Heating Tank Installer**
- **Land Surveyor**
- **Hairstylist**
- **Massage Therapist** (through provincial Massage Therapy Association).

Skilled Trades

PEI oversees both compulsory and designated trades. ApprenticeshipPEI manages training standards—certification is required to legally practice .

Non-Regulated but Industry-Recognized Professions

These include roles like Reiki, reflexology, aromatherapy, coaching, sound healing, makeup artistry, and other holistic practices. These fields lack government regulation but often follow insurance and industry best-practice standards .

Quick-Reference Table

Category	Regulated in PEI?	Requires Certification/Licence?
Medicine / Allied Health	✅ Yes	✅ Yes (regulated by authority)
ECE / Early Learning	✅ Yes	✅ Yes
Engineering / Architecture	✅ Yes	✅ Yes
Lawyer, CPA, Agrologist	✅ Yes	✅ Yes
Hairstylist, Paramedic, etc.	✅ Yes	✅ Yes
Massage Therapy (Association)	✅ Yes	✅ Yes (provincial membership)
Wellness & Creative Fields	❌ No	✅ Optional (for credibility/insurance)

Newfoundland & Labrador

Regulated Professions & Trades in Newfoundland & Labrador

Compulsory Skilled Trades

Under the *Apprenticeship and Certification Act*, NL currently has five compulsory trades requiring certification to legally work in them :

- Construction Electrician
- Residential Electrician
- Boom Truck Operator
- Mobile Crane Operator
- Tower Crane Operator

Additionally, NL oversees 62 designated trades, with 43 offering training programs and most being eligible for Red Seal certification .

Health & Allied Health Professions

These professions require licensure through provincial regulatory bodies to legally practice :

Profession	Regulatory Body
Audiologist, Speech-Language	NL Council of Health Professionals
Medical Lab Technologist	NL Council of Health Professionals
Medical Radiation Technologist	CAMRT (Canadian Assoc.)

Profession	Regulatory Body
Midwife	NL Council of Health Professionals
Occupational Therapist	NL Occupational Therapy Board
Pharmacist / Pharmacy Technician	College of Pharmacy of NL / Pharmacy Board
Physician	College of Physicians & Surgeons of NL
Physiotherapist	NL College of Physiotherapists
Practical Nurse	College of Licensed Practical Nurses NL
Paramedic	NL Paramedicine Regulation
Respiratory Therapist	NL Council of Health Professionals
Registered Nurse / NP	College of Registered Nurses NL
Psychologist	NL Psychology Board
Social Worker	NL College of Social Workers

These roles **cannot legally practice or use protected titles without proper licensing**.

Education & Early Learning

- **K–12 Teachers** require certification through NL's Department of Education
- **Early Childhood Educators (ECEs)** need provincial registration

Yukon

Regulated Professions & Trades in Yukon

Apprenticeship & Trades

Yukon operates an apprenticeship system for 40 designated trades, overseen by the Apprenticeship Training Act under the Department of Education . Many of these align with Red Seal trades recognized nationally .

Examples include:

- Electrician (Construction & Industrial)
- Plumber
- Heavy Equipment & Truck & Transport Technicians
- Cook, Baker, Cabinetmaker, Carpenter, Welder
- Hairstylist (licensed trade)
- Gasfitter, Refrigeration & Air Conditioning Mechanic
- Steamfitter/Pipefitter, Sheet Metal Worker, Machinist, etc. All require a multi-level apprenticeship (e.g. 1,600–1,800 hours per level + school time) .

Upon completion, apprentices earn a Certificate of Qualification, with Red Seal endorsement upon passing the interprovincial exam .

Regulated Professions Not Covered in Trades

While comprehensive data on non-trade professions (like health, legal, engineering) isn't centrally listed for Yukon, here's a general insight:

- Professions such as **nursing, teaching, engineering, or health care** follow provincial or national licensing models.
- **Electricians and other classified trades** are required to hold a Certificate of Qualification .

For other professions, Yukon often follows national or interprovincial standards regarding certification, registration, and privilege to practise.

What This Means for Course Creators

Category	Yukon Status	Requirements for Training Programs
Apprenticeship Trades	✅ Regulated (Certificate + Red Seal)	Must follow apprenticeship curriculum and certification
Non-trade Regulated Professions	⚠️ Likely regulated	Must comply with national professional standards
Unregulated Fields	✖️ Not regulated	Free to design outcome-based programs—but maintain clarity, ethics, and professional structure

Northwest Territories

Apprenticeship Trades

NWT's Apprenticeship, Trade and Occupation Certification (ATOC) program manages 43 designated trades and 17 occupations. Major Red Seal trades include:

- Electrician (construction & industrial)
- Plumber / Steamfitter / Pipefitter
- Carpenter / Cabinetmaker
- Heavy Equipment & Truck Mechanic
- Welder / Sheet Metal Worker
- Hairstylist
- Cook / Baker
- Millwright / Industrial Mechanic
- Aircraft Mechanic (federal jurisdiction)

All require apprenticeship plus interprovincial Red Seal or NWT certification to practice legally.

Regulated Health & Social Services

Under NWT's Professional Licensing Act, the Department of Health & Social Services licenses:

- Physicians, Dentists, Dental Hygienists/Therapists
- Nurses (RPN, LPN), Midwives, Paramedics
- Pharmacists, Optometrists
- Psychologists, Social Workers, Naturopaths, Dental Therapists
- Ophthalmic Medical Professionals, Veterinarians, Licensed Practical Nurses

These titles can only be used by licensed professionals.

Other Regulated Occupations

Several regulated roles require permits or certification by NWT government departments:

- Private Investigators, Security Guards
- Water/Wastewater Operators
- Pesticide/Petroleum Technicians
- Building Officials & Licence-to-Practice roles (e.g., Crane Operators)
- Funeral Directors, Pawnbrokers, Real Estate Agents, Insurance Professionals

Non-Regulated Training Fields

Fields like Reiki, Reflexology, Massage Therapy (unless association-regulated), Coaching, Aromatherapy, Makeup Artistry, and Energy Healing are not provincially regulated, though they may require industry best-practices and insurance compliance.

Summary Table

Category	Regulated in NWT?	Requires Certification/Licence?
Apprenticeship Trades	✓ Yes	✓ Yes (apprenticeship + Red Seal)
Health & Social Service Roles	✓ Yes	✓ Yes (licensed)
Other Licensed Occupations	✓ Yes	✓ Yes (permit/licence)
Wellness & Creative Fields	✗ No	✓ Optional (for credibility/insurance)

Nunavut

Regulated Professions & Trades in Nunavut

Apprenticeship & Trades (Nunavut Arctic College / Apprenticeship Unit)

Nunavut offers Red Seal apprenticeship programs in partnership with southern colleges—typically structured as:

- 3–4 year programs combining on-the-job training (1,500–6,240 hours depending on trade) and in-class technical training (about 240 hours/year)
- Examples include: Carpenter, Electrician, Plumber/Gasfitter, Oil Heat Systems Technician, Housing Maintainer. Apprentice must contract with an employer and pass progressive level exams to earn a Certificate of Qualification and optional Red Seal credential

Health & Licensed Professionals

Nunavut governs several health professions through licensing authorities:

- Physicians: Must hold the Licentiate of the Medical Council of Canada plus certification from national bodies (CMP, CFPC) to practice
- Nurses (RNs & LPNs): Licensed by the College and Association of Nurses of the Northwest Territories & Nunavut (CANNN) under territorial legislation
- Other regulated health roles include: Dental professionals, Naturopaths, Midwives, Pharmacists, Optometrists, Psychologists, Social Workers, and

Veterinarians—each licensed via the Professional Licensing Office

Legal & Other Regulated Roles

- Lawyers are regulated by the Law Society of Nunavut
- Municipal staff & field workers may receive training through the Nunavut Municipal Training Organization at Arctic College

Unregulated—but Common in Private Training

Fields that are not provincially regulated in Nunavut include:

- Reiki, Aromatherapy, Reflexology
- Coaching, NLP, Hypnotherapy
- Massage Therapy (not yet regulated)
- Makeup artistry, Sound Healing, Energy Healing

These areas are often taught privately and rely on industry standards and liability insurance, but do not require government oversight.

Why This Matters for Course Creators

- Apprenticeship trades must align with exact curricula, hold official apprenticeship contracts, and meet requirements for exams and Red Seal credentials.
- Health and licensed professions: Programs need structured curriculum and must guide students toward territorial licensing.
- Unregulated fields: Educators have freedom in course design, with emphasis on professionalism, course integrity, and student protection.

Summary Table – Nunavut

Category	Regulated?	Requires Certification/Licence
Apprenticeship Trades	✓ Yes	✓ Yes (Certificate + Red Seal)
Physicians, Nursing, Allied Health	✓ Yes	✓ Yes (Territorial license)
Dental, Midwife, Psychologist	✓ Yes	✓ Yes
Law (Lawyers)	✓ Yes	✓ Yes
Town Staff / Fire & Rescue	⚠ Licensed training	✓ Yes (Municipal certificates)
Wellness Macrobiology & Arts	✗ No	✓ Optional (insurance standards)

GLOBAL

USA

Occupational Licensing in the U.S.

1. ### State-by-State Regulation
   Each state has its own list of licensed occupations,
   overseen by boards or licensing departments. For instance:
   - Texas: TDLR regulates massage therapists,
     cosmetologists, midwives, dietitians, electricians,
     and more
   - Florida: DBPR licenses barbers, real estate agents,
     veterinarians, tattoo artists, spas, and more

2. ### Licensed Fields Often Include
   - ### Health & Allied Health: Nurses,
     physicians, PTs, etc.
   - ### Skilled Trades: Electricians, plumbers,
     cosmetologists, barbers
   - ### Property & Legal: Real estate, appraisal,
     notary, private investigators, engineers
   - ### Wellness & Body Arts: Tattooing, body
     piercing, massage therapy, esthetics

3. ### Latency & Licensing Burden
   Licensing burdens vary widely—California and Utah are
   known for particularly restrictive systems, while Kansas
   and Missouri are more liberal.

4. ### Portability Issues
   Licenses often don't transfer across state lines. To address
   this, some professions (like nursing) use "compacts" that
   allow multistate licensure.

Key Categories and Examples

Health & Allied Health Professions

- Regulated in every state. Includes physicians, RNs/PAs, massage therapists (in many states), physical therapists, speech therapists, paramedics, midwives, and more.
- Often require accredited education, exams, supervised hours, and renewal CLE.

Licensed Trades & Personal Services

- ## Cosmetologists, Estheticians, Barbers: Require training, exams, and license renewal.
- ## Tradespeople (electricians, plumbers, HVAC, auto mechanics): Apprentice-based systems regulated by state workforce agencies.
- ## Massage Therapy: State-regulated in many jurisdictions, mirroring vocational licensing.
- ## Tattoo Artists, Piercers: Often regulated by health or licensing boards.

Business, Property & Legal Professionals

- ## Real Estate Agents/Brokers, Appraisers, Insurance Agents, CPAs, Architects, Engineers, Private Investigators, Auctioneers, etc.: Each field has licensing exams and approved training programs.

Wellness & Coaching Fields

- Largely **unregulated**: Reiki, life coaching, NLP, crystal healing, aromatherapy.
- Some states regulate **massage, midwifery, hypnotherapy**. For example, Texas regulates massage therapists and midwives via TDLR.

Implications for Your Readers

Field Type	Regulation in U.S.?	Training Required
Health/allied professions	✅ Yes – state-level licensing	Accredited education, supervised hours, state exams
Skilled trades & personal services	✅ Many regulated (varies by state)	Apprenticeship or licensed training + exams
Property, business, legal professionals	✅ Yes – licensing exams/certification	Approved courses, professional exams
Wellness & creative fields	✖ Mostly unregulated nationally	Voluntary certification; insurance depends on standards

How to Navigate State Licensing

- Use state government "Professional Boards" or "Licensing Departments" to find the full list for each state.
- Check training requirements, exam prep, required hours, and continuing education.
- Look into interstate compacts for fields like nursing and counseling .
- Stay alert for state updates—some are reducing licensing burdens (e.g. Nevada recently reviewed its licensing lists).

United Kingdom

Regulated Routes in the UK

Regulated Professions (using protected titles or requiring licence)

The UK's *Professional Qualifications Act* outlines occupations that are legally regulated—meaning you must meet qualification/experience requirements and register with the appropriate authority to use protected titles.

Key examples include:

Healthcare & Care Professions (regulated via HCPC, GMC, etc.)

- Physiotherapist, Paramedic, Radiographer, Dietitian, Biomedical Scientist, Speech & Language Therapist, Psychologist, Chiropodist/Podiatrist, Operating Department Practitioner
- Doctors (General Medical Council)
- Chiropractor (General Chiropractic Council)

Education

- Early years practitioners (Level 2 & 3), school teachers, college lecturers (each regulated through different bodies depending on region)

Legal, Technical & Professional

- Architects, engineers, lawyers, social workers, accountants, surveyors, vets, pharmacists, and more—all require registration/licensing under national or devolved regulations

Apprenticeships & Skilled Trades

The UK offers formal apprenticeships from Level 2 (equivalent to GCSE) up to Level 7 (master's degree). Employers like the British Army, BBC, and BAE Systems participate—offering hands-on training alongside academic credentials.

You'll find programs in:

- Construction and engineering trades
- Healthcare (e.g. nursing, paramedics)
- Digital, IT, management, finance
- Policy, regulatory affairs (Level 7)

Apprenticeship standards are nationally approved, ensuring consistency across regions.

Unregulated or Voluntarily Regulated Fields

Fields like psychotherapy, counselling, life coaching, Reiki, makeup artistry, massage therapy, etc., are not legally protected titles, though reputable associations (e.g. BACP) offer voluntary accreditation.

Notably, psychotherapy and counselling are under increasing political pressure to become statutory in England.

What This Means for Your Readers

Type of Field	Requires Legal Regulation?	Training Program Needs
HCPC/GMC-level Healthcare Professions	☑ Yes	Accredited curriculum, registration/licensing, regulated practicum requirements
Apprenticeship Trades & Professions	☑ Yes	Must follow approved apprenticeship standards across Levels 2–7
Protected Professional Titles	☑ Yes	Degree or accredited training + regulatory body registration
Unregulated Wellness Programs	✖ No (but may have industry standards)	Flexibility in curriculum design, assurance via voluntary certification, clear course structure

Australia

AU Regulated Professions & Training in Australia

Health Professions (National Scheme via AHPRA)

A national system under the Australian Health Practitioner Regulation Agency (Ahpra) oversees 16 health professions, including:

- Medical practitioners, nurses and midwives, dental practitioners, pharmacists, physiotherapists, occupational therapists, psychologists, chiropractors, optometrists, osteopaths, podiatrists, paramedics, Chinese medicine practitioners, Aboriginal and Torres Strait Islander health practitioners, and medical radiation practitioners

These professions require registration, accredited education, ongoing professional development, and are legally protected titles.

Apprenticeships & Trades (VET & RTO System)

Australia uses a dual system combining on-the-job apprenticeship/traineeship with off-the-job vocational training through Registered Training Organisations (RTOs):

- Common trades include electricians, plumbers, carpenters, welders, mechanics, chefs, gasfitters, hairstylists, and more.
- RTOs are overseen by the Australian Skills Quality Authority (ASQA) in most states or corresponding state bodies in WA and Victoria.
- Apprenticeships lead to formal national qualifications and often include Red Seal registration for trades.

Higher-Level Apprenticeships and Professionals

- Higher apprenticeship levels range from Certificate II to Master's-level (Level 7) qualifications, including roles in digital, management, finance, and health sectors .
- Engineering and psychology require professional accreditation (e.g., via Engineers Australia or Psychology Board of Australia), alongside university degrees.

Unregulated Fields & Private Training

Fields not regulated by government law include:

- Wellness and creative industries like Reiki, coaching, aromatherapy, sound healing, makeup artistry, etc. Still, educators operate under:
- RTO regulations if offering accredited qualifications
- Industry best practices, insurance, and voluntary certifications

Summary Table

Category	Regulated?	Requires Registered Training Programs?
Ahpra-registered health professions	☑ Yes	Yes—university degree or accredited program + AHPRA registration
Apprenticeship and skilled trades	☑ Yes	Yes—RTO-led apprenticeships, national qualifications
Higher-level vocational qualifications	☑ Yes	Yes—RTO-delivered, can range up to master's equivalent
Engineering, psychology, legal, finance	☑ Yes	Yes—accredited degrees + professional registration
Unregulated wellness & creative fields	✖ No	Not required—but benefit from RTO structure or private curriculum

Africa

South Africa

Regulated professions are governed by statutory professional councils—for example:

- **Health Professions Council of South Africa (HPCSA)** regulates 12 categories like doctors, therapists, dentists, pharmacists, psychologists, and more. Use of protected titles requires registration and accredited training.
- **Engineering Council of South Africa (ECSA)** oversees professional engineers.
- Additional statutory bodies include the South African Pharmacy Council, Nursing Council (SANC), built environment councils, legal authorities, etc.

Key takeaway for course creators:

Courses in fields like medicine, engineering, architecture, or counselling must align with council-accredited curricula and prepare students for mandatory registration and licensing.

Kenya

While not heavily focused on profession-specific regulation, Kenya has stricter oversight in trades and markets:

- The **Kenya Bureau of Standards (KEBS)** enforces product and industrial quality standards.
- **Capital Markets Authority (CMA)** regulates financial services—namely brokers and forex.

Regarding professions like medicine, law, or engineering, regulation exists but standards vary by body and region.

Key takeaway:

Courses tied to trades, manufacturing, finance, or finance-related roles may require alignment with KEBS/CMA. Courses in other professional fields should follow governance by relevant professional councils/institutions.

Other English-Speaking Countries (e.g., Nigeria, Ghana, Uganda)

Common themes:

- Health and engineering professions require training accredited by bodies like Medical and Dental Councils, Nursing Councils, and Engineering Registration Boards.
- Legal, accounting, architecture—likewise regulated by Law Societies, Institutes of Chartered Accountants, Architects' Councils.
- Vocational training, small trades, and wellness services (e.g., Reiki, coaching, spiritual ministries) tend to be unregulated—but providers often opt for private certification, insurance, and professional association (e.g., beauty schools, vocational institutes).

Overall Summary: Key Zones

Field Type	Regulated?	Notes for Course Creators
Medicine, Allied Health	☑ Yes	Requires accredited, council-approved curriculum
Engineering, Law, Finance	☑ Yes	Oversight by professional boards/regulatory bodies
Trades & Vocational Programs	⚠ Often yes	Standards vary by country and sector (e.g., Kenya Standards)
Wellness & Spiritual Training	✖ No	Private certification, insurance, and structure recommended

Bibliography

Government & Accreditation Bodies:

- Private Training Institutions Branch (PTIB), British Columbia – www.privatetraininginstitutions.gov.bc.ca
- Alberta Ministry of Advanced Education – www.alberta.ca/advanced-education.aspx
- Manitoba Advanced Education and Training – www.edu.gov.mb.ca
- Saskatchewan Ministry of Advanced Education – www.saskatchewan.ca/government/government-structure/ministries/advanced-education
- Ontario Ministry of Colleges and Universities – www.ontario.ca/page/ministry-colleges-universities
- Government of Canada – Post-Secondary Education – www.canada.ca/en/services/education/postsecondary.html
- U.S. Department of Education – www.ed.gov
- Higher Learning Commission (U.S.) – www.hlcommission.org
- Ofqual – UK Office of Qualifications and Examinations Regulation – www.gov.uk/government/organisations/ofqual
- Australian Skills Quality Authority (ASQA) – www.asqa.gov.au
- Council on Higher Education (South Africa) – www.che.ac.za

Legal & Operational Resources:

- City of Kelowna Business Licensing Department –
  www.kelowna.ca
- WorkSafeBC – www.worksafebc.com
- DataWitness – www.datawitness.com (Digital Records
  Storage)
- Small Business BC – www.smallbusinessbc.ca
- Canada Revenue Agency – www.canada.ca/en/revenue-
  agency.html

Adult Education & Curriculum Design:

- Knowles, Malcolm. *The Adult Learner: A Neglected Species.*
  Houston: Gulf Publishing, 1984.
- Bloom, Benjamin. *Taxonomy of Educational Objectives: The
  Classification of Educational Goals.* New York: Longmans,
  Green, 1956.
- Wiggins, Grant, and Jay McTighe. *Understanding by Design.*
  ASCD, 2005.

Personal Experience:

- Santego, Constance. Based on 14+ years of experience as
  a private college owner and post-secondary educator in
  British Columbia.

About The Author

Dr. Constance Santego, Ph.D., DNM
Author • Educator • Natural Medicine Doctor • School Founder

Dr. Constance Santego is a visionary educator, bestselling author, and respected expert in holistic healing and natural medicine. With a Ph.D. and Doctorate in Natural Medicine, she brings over two decades of experience empowering others through education, transformation, and intuitive development.

In 1999, what began as a dream to open a healing center in Kelowna, British Columbia, quickly became a calling to teach. A surprise conversation at city hall led to the founding of her first school—one that would go on to gain government accreditation, launch hundreds of careers, and change the lives of both students and clients across Canada.

As the former owner and operator of an accredited private post-secondary college, Constance knows firsthand what it takes to create, run, and sustain educational programs rooted in ethics, excellence, and purpose. She has developed and delivered dozens of certification courses in natural and energy medicine, aesthetics, business, and personal growth.

Now the author of over 40 published titles—including both non-fiction and spiritual fiction—Dr. Santego continues to share her legacy through writing, speaking, and course creation. Her mission is to light the path for others who are ready to share their knowledge and build something meaningful—whether that's a single course or an entire school.

When she's not writing or teaching, you can find her in beautiful British Columbia, enjoying time with her family, mentoring emerging educators, or envisioning her next creation.

Message from the Author

Dr. Constance Santego

If you're holding this book in your hands, chances are you have a calling—not just to help others, but to *teach* them. Maybe you've mastered a skill, developed a method, or gained wisdom through life experience… and now, you feel the nudge to share it.

I want you to know something important: **you don't need permission to become a teacher—only a commitment to do it with clarity, ethics, and heart**.

This book is my offering to those walking a path I know well. I wrote it not just to share what worked, but also what didn't. The successes, yes—but also the stumbles, the legal lessons, the zoning nightmares, the audits, and the moments I almost gave up.

And yet… I didn't.
I went on to become a Doctor of Natural Medicine, a bestselling author, and someone who now gets to teach across books, courses, and workshops. Not because it was easy—but because it was *worth it*.

You have something valuable to offer. This world doesn't need more perfection—it needs more people willing to lead from experience.

So take the leap. Teach with integrity. And build something that not only teaches—but transforms.

With gratitude and belief in your vision,
Dr. Constance Santego
Ph.D., DNM, College Founder & Educator

ALSO AVAILABLE

The *Train the Trainer* program was created by **Dr. Constance Santego** for her daughter, **Alicia Brummet's** school, 24 Karat Beauty Academy, after seeing firsthand the gaps in instructor preparation across many beauty and wellness training institutes. Alicia often worked for schools that hired recent graduates with little to no teaching experience—and in some cases, less than a few months of hands-on practitioner training.

Determined to raise the standards and ensure future educators are equipped with the skills, ethics, and structure they need to truly support their students, Dr. Santego developed this comprehensive program. *Train the Trainer* is rooted in real-world experience, industry expectations, and the deep belief that every student deserves a qualified, confident teacher.

Train the Trainer – 24 Karat Beauty Academy
https://www.24karatbeauty.com/trainthetrainer

PLAY THE GAME *IKONA* – DISCOVER YOUR INNER GENIE

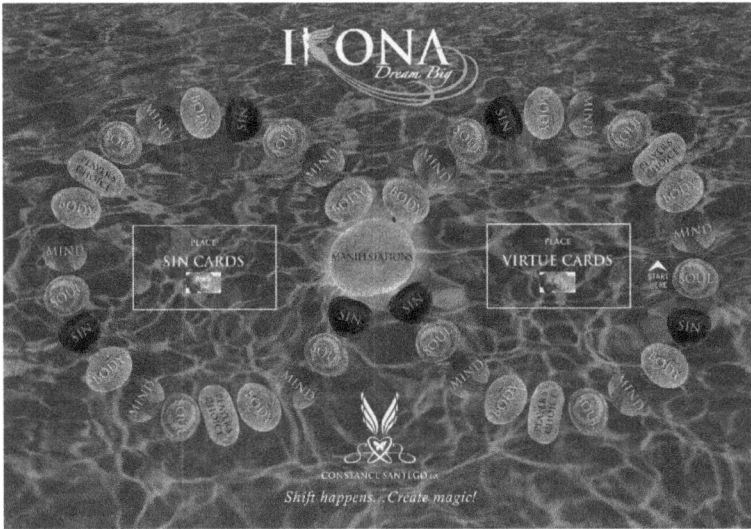

For additional information on

Constance Santego's

wide range of Motivational Products, Coaching Sessions, Spiritual Retreats,
Live Events and Educational Programs

Go to

www.ConstanceSantego.ca

Follow on Instagram - Constance_Santego and
Facebook - constancesantegoo

Subscribe and receive Free Information and Meditations on my
YouTube Channel - Constance Santego